SCARE-IZONA

SCARE-IZONA

A Travel Guide to Arizona's Spookiest Spots

Katie Mullaly
and J. Patrick Ohlde

Schiffer Publishing Ltd®

4880 Lower Valley Road, Atglen, Pennsylvania 19310

DEDICATIONS

For my husband Mikal, and my children, Seamus and Liam, who are the center of my universe.
For my wife Ashley. Without her love, patience, and understanding this book would never have happened.

Designed by Mark David Bowyer
Type set in Demon / NewsGoth BT

ISBN: 978-0-7643-2844-2
Printed in China

Schiffer Books are available at special discounts for bulk purchases for sales promotions or premiums. Special editions, including personalized covers, corporate imprints, and excerpts can be created in large quantities for special needs. For more information contact the publisher:

Published by Schiffer Publishing Ltd.
4880 Lower Valley Road
Atglen, PA 19310
Phone: (610) 593-1777; Fax: (610) 593-2002
E-mail: Info@schifferbooks.com

For the largest selection of fine reference books on this and related subjects, please visit our web site at
www.schifferbooks.com
We are always looking for people to write books on new and related subjects. If you have an idea for a book please contact us at the above address.

This book may be purchased from the publisher.
Include $3.95 for shipping.
Please try your bookstore first.
You may write for a free catalog.

In Europe, Schiffer books are distributed by
Bushwood Books
6 Marksbury Ave.
Kew Gardens
Surrey TW9 4JF England
Phone: 44 (0) 20 8392-8585; Fax: 44 (0) 20 8392-9876
E-mail: info@bushwoodbooks.co.uk
Website: www.bushwoodbooks.co.uk
Free postage in the U.K., Europe; air mail at cost.

CONTENTS

Acknowledgments

God, for providing an afterlife in the first place;

Ashley Ohlde, for leading us to this opportunity and for her continued patience and support;

Peyton Perks, for being enormously cheerful and encouraging;

Lyle and Belinda Ohlde, for a solid upbringing and a really comfy place to stay;

Kim and Jack Alfred, for the comfy place to stay on weekends;

Mikal Mullaly, for his moderate patience, keen driving skills, and superlative event coordination;

Seamus and Liam, for being perfect little gentlemen (most of the time), and also for carrying the equipment;

Dinah Roseberry and Schiffer Publishing, for giving us a chance;

Bill Everist, for his infinite wisdom of all things paranormal and for participation in this book;

Jaci Vigil, for her meticulous and sometimes brutally honest proofreading skills;

Nicole Purdue, for sharing experiences and being awesome;

Andrea and Cory, for their covert operations;

Rebeca and Cecilia Cardenas, for their enthusiastic participation;

Tony and Becka Trevino, for holding down the fort...and then cleaning, organizing, and remodeling the fort;

Maureen, Diane, and NSYNC, for all the sparkly summer fun;

Zack Alfred, for carrying dressers on a dime;

John, for pulling me from the jaws of that wolf...I never actually thanked you for that, did I? Better late than never, eh?

Dan, Jenny, Davin, and Nathan, for all the late night card games;

Linda, Felicia, and Leslie, for all the pageants and pizza;

All of our family and friends, for their encouragement and support;

Rhonda, for watching the kids, the house, and the dogs;

To everyone who helped us above and beyond the call of duty, particularly:

Allison from Hotel Congress; Herb, Jennifer, Mike, and Amber from the Fox Theatre; Michael Monti from Monti's; Gavin from Casey Moore's; Everyone at 22nd Street Antiques; Marti, Kim, Sharon, Rick, and Sandy from Colossal Cave Mountain Park; Rosalie and Dom from Noftsger Hill Inn; Anne from Connor Hotel; and to everyone else who contributed in any way to the completion of this book.

FOREWORD

I t's always good to see your students succeed in a curricu-
lum-related venture. Such is the case with this new edition
of ghost lore from the wild west of Arizona. As you venture
through the pages of this book, you will not only see a suggested methodology in approaching your practical search into
the history of Arizona, but also a personal accountability of the
authors' experiences.

What makes the book unique is that you are not only provided
with the alleged history to these sites, but also the personal accounts of Katie and Patrick. And although it would be impractical
to think that you would experience the exact same thing, it at
least provides a basis for what you might anticipate.

In a contemporary society where "ghost hunting" has become
a part-time, favorite weekend adventure, this book provides an
oasis of excellent sites for exploration throughout the state, many
of which I had the good fortune of exploring with the authors as
students of my class in Paranormal Psychology.

From Monti's La Casa Vieja Restaurant in Tempe to the Jerome Grand Hotel, the Bisbee Inn/Hotel La More, the Oliver House, Big Nose Kate's and more, these accounts brought back numerous memories of class experiences that assured an adventure similar to capturing a piece of the "old west." And yet, these experiences were just my own and others.

So saddle-up, your piece of the old west is still out there waiting for you. Wrap your sense of adventure around this book and take a look at what's out there in your past...and future.

—William G. Everist, M.A.

Instructor of Paranormal Psychology

INTRODUCTION

What happens after we die? That is a question that everyone has asked themselves at one time or another. Do we float away to a better place or simply cease to exist? Do our spirits stay moored to places we loved or hated the most while alive, or do we vanish into thin air? There are those who think they have the answers and those who don't believe that the answer exists. There are also the kinds of people who want to test their own personal endurance of fear, or experience their own brief connection with the paranormal, so that they will have a spooky story to tell their friends when the lights are out. Everyone will develop their own concept of the afterlife or lack thereof, and we are certainly not in the business of lengthy, heated existential debates with hypertensive orators bent on cramming their notions down the throats of anyone within earshot. We already have our beliefs firmly in place, and we have the experience and evidence to back them. We crave the adrenaline rush of capturing that anomalous photo, or hearing the disembodied cries upon playback of the voice recorder, and we want to give that experience to everyone who shares our passion on any level. This book is intended for the thrill-seeking folks who want to learn the ropes of paranormal investigation — and to have fun doing it.

The world of the paranormal is as vast as it is crowded. As we have established, most of us are concerned on some level with what happens to us once we die. It is natural to take some interest in whatever evidence there might be for and against an afterlife. From the hardcore skeptic who feels that death is the final word, to the hardcore believer who is certain the spirit endures, there are as many beliefs and conclusions drawn on the subject as there are people inquiring about it. That being the case, the ordinary person who doesn't devote every waking second to research on the subject can be left feeling even more confused and befuddled than before. It's a complex subject, and while there are no easy answers, the study of it can certainly be made a bit easier. The aim of this book is to provide the casual investigator the means to look into some of the experiences the paranormal has to offer without requiring an advanced degree in an obscure study or the feelings of ridiculousness that we are often taught to feel when curious about ghosts and hauntings.

We will use simplified methods to allow weekend ghost-hunters to get a feel for what it's like to investigate ghosts on their own terms and in their own time. We'll advise about the dos and don'ts of planning and implementing one's own casual investigation. We will tell you the best places to go and how to get there. We understand that breaking into this sort of study can be scarier than the ghosts that you will be studying, and that is okay — Wailing Bansidhe is here for you. You don't have to feel like some kind of a freak to do this; you just need an open mind, some resources, your toothbrush, and directions. We are already packed, so buckle up — it's going to be a scary ride!

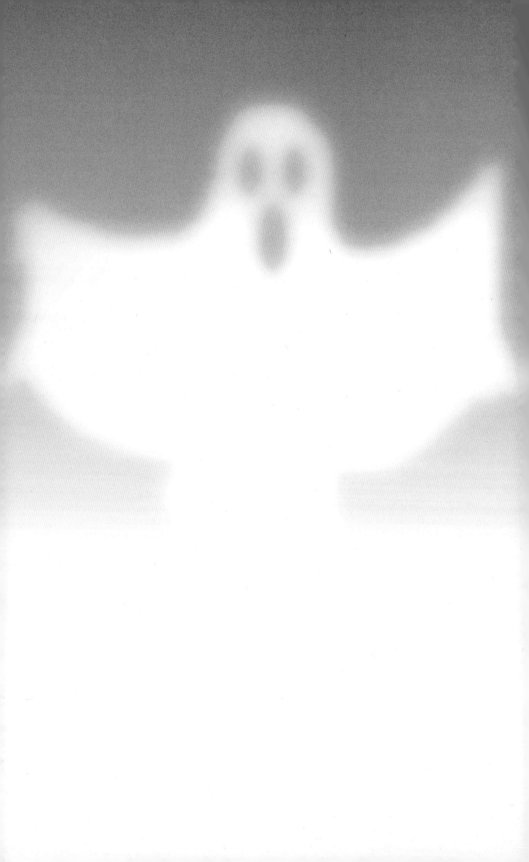

SECTION ONE:
WHAT TO KNOW BEFORE YOU GO

DO GHOSTS EXIST ?

Absolutely. Can we prove that? Absolutely not. If we were able to prove the existence of ghosts, then this book would serve no purpose. The thrill of ghost-hunting is the idea that you may, for just one moment, cross the blurred line between the living and the dead, and to capture that moment in some tangible medium (i.e. photographic anomaly, electronic voice phenomenon). Naysayers the world over maintain that we merely stop existing when we die, but thousands of tales of unexplained personal experiences and first-hand accounts of apparitions and otherworldly encounters tell a different story. Perhaps there is not yet any concrete evidence to support the existence of an afterlife, but are all of those people really wrong? We doubt it.

While the scientific world requires absolutes when determining the existence of ghosts, we believe that nothing speaks louder than real people with real experiences. Every person has had an experience that he/she cannot explain, and every person loves to share those experiences with others who promise not to think the storyteller has lost his or her mind. We all know that ghosts exist in some capacity, but admitting a belief in the paranormal can be like admitting a belief in the Tooth Fairy. The interest in the paranormal stems from the very inability to prove the existence of much of it, and the mystery is what keeps us enthralled. The purpose of this guide is not to prove nor disprove the existence of ghosts, but rather to guide you, our esteemed reader, in the direction of determining that for yourself.

Why Arizona ?

Although Arizona wasn't officially made a state until February 14, 1912, one culture or another has occupied it for approximately 18,000 years. That is quite a lengthy time span for people to be living and dying in this particular corner of the world. Add to that the fact that many of these cultures were not necessarily neighborly with each other, and would have sooner slit the throats of an entire peaceful community rather than politely ask to borrow a cup of sugar. In the natural order of things, it is generally accepted that only the strongest should survive, and this natural selection has been augmented over the centuries by countless rock-throwing, hatchet-swinging, gun-toting militants looking for any and every opportunity for personal gain, without regard to destruction or consequence.

Nestled squarely in the bosom of the Wild West, there is not one square inch of this state that has not witnessed some form of deadly conflict, be it the result of wartime violence or the addled machinations of stagecoach robbing bandits and thieves. Some areas, particularly Tombstone and parts of Tucson, have certainly seen more than their fair share of raucous debauchery and flagrant disregard for life. Cattle rustling was an enormous problem, and one of the main offenders was a group referred to as The Cowboys. Operating in a large and powerful gang, The Cowboys made it their business to brazenly steal cattle, and then kill anyone who might have tried to stop them, and then kill another dozen or so otherwise uninvolved parties just for theatrics. Ranchers were forced to defend themselves by any means necessary while the unarmed citizens were usually caught in the crossfire. The remote landscape of this state is peppered with graveyards, many of which have long since been forgotten — swallowed by overgrowths of brush or washed away by flash flooding — allowing the unfortunate disruption of the final resting place of countless decedents. Many graves are unmarked and unknown, and many of their occupants may not even realize they are dead.

As the state moved forward with technology, the transition was not always smooth. The untapped land in Arizona was rich in mineral ore and the establishment of a mine attracted countless men hoping to find work and create better lives for their families. Sadly, the very nature of mining also brings with it the virtual guarantee that lives will be lost in the process and families will be forever marred by the loss of everything they hoped for and held dear. Jerome and Bisbee are two towns built around the mining boom that suffered such immeasurable loss through mining tragedies, that the impact has left many of those miners to navigate an endless and confusing quest for eternal peace.

Even today, circumstance and tragedy continue to add layers to an already well-established population of hauntings and apparitions, and based on its very nature it is not a cycle that is likely to stop any time soon. The long held belief that haunting activity is a rarity, reserved only for darkly shrouded mansions with long driveways and creepy caretakers, is rapidly vanishing. Replacing this outdated notion is the comfortable sense that we are sharing our space with those that have gone before us, and with whom we may still be able to remain in contact, even if only through fleeting glances, barely audible whispers, and the chilling touch of a disembodied hand.

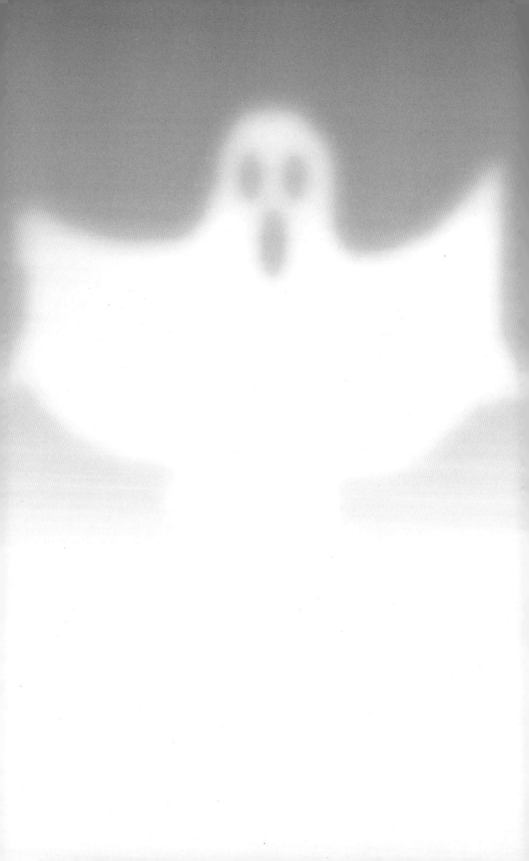

WHO ARE WE, ANYWAY ?

So all of this is well and good, but what makes us so special we should write a book about it? Credibility is a big thing in this field. Given its nature, it tends to attract all manner of characters to its study. It gets to a point where it feels like a badly played game of telephone, where the original information gets more than a little muddled by the time it reaches your ear. We are the members of Wailing Bansidhe Investigations, an Arizona-based team that has spent a great deal of time and energy trying to put the "normal" back into paranormal investigation. While there are more members than the three of us, the collective "we" in this case consists of the core founding members: Katie Mullaly, Mikal Mullaly, and J. Patrick Ohlde. Because we believe in knowing who is selling you the bill of goods as well as the full inventory, we'll toss out our credentials:

Katie Mullaly — She has been involved in paranormal investigation in some form or another since she could walk and talk. What started as a childhood interest has grown into a serious pursuit that led to her intensely studying the subject.

From courses at the collegiate level to taking part in professional investigations, Katie has done a bit of everything. Although she maintains that anything is possible, she prefers to be regarded as an open-minded skeptic.

Mikal Mullaly — The photographer, tech guy, event planner, and also the resident skeptic. Even after having experiences of his own, Mikal maintains that he must see proof and, in doing so, keeps the rest of us honest.

J. Patrick Ohlde — He holds a Bachelor's degree in Psychology from the University of Arizona. During his study, he took classes involving the paranormal and became involved with Pima Community College's paranormal investigation team, where he participated in many investigations around the state. He is open-minded, but tends to need to see some proof as well.

THE INVESTIGATION: WHAT'S INVOLVED ?

So how does one actually investigate a haunting? In addition to having the right tools and the terminology — all of which we'll tell you about in this section — the investigation has to have some sort of a backbone; otherwise you have investigators wandering around all loosey goosey, bumping into one another. For this methodology, we have chosen to use a sort of abbreviated, casual form of the method employed by Gertrude Schmeidler, a well-known and well-respected pioneer in the field of ESP (extra sensory perception) and PK (psychokinesis) research, as well as haunting phenomena.

The way the method works is to take a group of people, often referred to as sensitives, into a haunted place, provide them with floor plans and notepads, and send them on a walk-through of the area. During this walk-through, the sensitives are not permitted to speak to one another and only one person is allowed in a room at any given time. The sensitives should not have any advance knowledge of the activity in the place or its history. You want as blank a slate as possible to keep the findings from being corrupted. Obviously, drugs and alcohol are also a big no-no unless you want any gathered data to be useless and discredited. Keep in mind that when we refer to "sensitives," we are not suggesting that it is a requirement that the investigation be limited to people who claim some sixth sense type of ability. Anyone can, and should, participate in the walk-through to allow a broader scope of impressions and sensations.

While on the walk-through, the sensitives will make note of any feelings or sensations they get and indicate its location on the floor plan. They mark the exact spot and use some descriptor word to illustrate what they are feeling (hot, cold, dizzy, angry, short of breath, etc.). Obviously, if anything is seen or heard, note of it should also be made. If the investigation is one in which an overnight stay is included, the sensitive should also keep a dream journal during the night. If they have any odd or vivid dreams, those should be jotted down with as much detail as possible. Nothing should be left out when dream journaling because even the tiniest detail can result in a significant hit if experienced by more than one person in the group.

After the walk-through or overnight stay is complete, the investigators then interview the staff, management, or patrons available who have experienced things over the years and see if anything they noted during the walk-throughs or in their dreams matches up with previous reports. If a spot you've marked corresponds with a spot previously reported, you have a direct hit. General impressions in the same room as reported activity provide a softer hit, but are worth noting anyway.

If one were to do this scientifically, the rules must be rigidly followed and the data would be analyzed statistically, usually through a chi square test, to find if the results are significant.

For our purposes, both because this is a resource for the unini-tiated or casual investigator, and because we honestly would rather not direct our time into gathering all kinds of statistical data when the thrill of the experience is vastly more exciting to us, statistical tests will not be necessary and the rules you choose to follow are up to you (provided, of course, that they are within the generally accepted boundaries of ghost-hunting, and not made up on the spot to accommodate some absurd and unreasonable whim).

In a general sense, in order to have anything slightly credible to talk about, it is important to go into the situation without prior knowledge of activity and events reported in the past, and to remain sober for the investigation. Any drug or alcohol use immediately makes the findings suspect. There is harsh enough criticism of paranormal findings as it is without throwing the "Yeah, but were you high?" argument in the mix.

It's also important to remember that hunting for ghosts in the real world is not like it is in the movies. As exciting as it would be, you aren't going to be pursued down a hallway by a floating green slime monster and statues won't come to life and try to drown you. Sorry. The actual process is a bit quieter and more internal than all of that, and sometimes you simply come up empty. While walking through rooms and jotting down impressions and feelings isn't as gripping as jumping through inter-dimensional vortexes in an effort to get your daughter out of the TV set, it is still very rewarding to score a direct hit or see an apparition float by.

Our recommendation when doing this on your own is to try to talk to the management of the hotel or restaurant you're investigating to see what they are comfortable allowing you to do. It can keep you out of trouble and also may get you access you might not normally have. If the management is not interested in indulging your paranormal fancy, there is still plenty of rules-following fun you can have in the areas to which you do have access.

The Tools...

No investigation would be complete without the necessary tools to collect the intended data. There are numerous tools that can be used in the course of an investigation, ranging from dowsing rods to infrared cameras. Of those that are appropriate for a paranormal investigation, there are no right or wrong tools, and each investigator tends to have an affinity for a particular tool. There are some tools that are easier to use and more portable than others. For our purposes, we will be using the following equipment. All of these are handheld, non-invasive, and require no set up or break down. They also have the added advantage of fitting neatly into a medium-sized purse or shoulder bag... for the ghost-hunters that prefer to be more discreet about their experience. Any bag that can be used to sneak soda and candy into a movie theater will be more than adequate in carrying the following tools:

Camera – If you can choose only one tool for your investigation, it should be either a 35mm or a digital camera. Cameras not only capture and preserve the moment for posterity, they also allow date and time settings and, perhaps most impressive, they are frequently able to capture things that are not visible to the naked eye. Digital cameras have the added advantage of immediate gratification. There is nothing more satisfying on an investigation than being able to look at the display screen of the image you just took and say, "Hey guys! Come take a look at this!"

EMF detector – As the name suggests, this device detects and measures EMF, otherwise known as electromagnetic fields. This tool is important because it allows the investigator to locate pockets of electromagnetic energy and determine their sources. Most electronic devices give off electromagnetic fields of varying intensity. Even people give off some degree of electromagnetism. All of these can be monitored with an EMF detector. EMF detectors can serve to both support a haunting, as well as pinpoint other possible causes of otherwise unexplained activity. EMF detectors are available at most electronics stores and are relatively inexpensive.

Voice recorder – As with a camera, a voice recorder has the capability of capturing sounds that may not be audible to the human ear. During an investigation, a recorder can either be used to pose questions to the alleged apparition to see if any response is evident at playback, or it can be used during the normal interaction of an investigation without making any specific attempts at direct contact. The playback can then be reviewed for any sounds or voices that were not heard at the time of the investigation. It should be noted that these recordings can be very difficult to substantiate, and should not be the sole source of evidence. Much in the same way that a lie detector test is not admissible in court but can point one in the right direction, the EVP recording can support findings, but should never be the basis of those findings.

Digital thermometer – Since many apparitions and hauntings involve both hot and cold spots, it is only fitting to use a small, digital thermometer. A thermometer can be used to monitor temperature changes, and is ideally combined simultaneously with data from other instruments. During an investigation, it can be easy to let your mind trick you into thinking that you are experiencing temperature fluctuations of otherworldly origin. With the thermometer, you don't have to guess and you have a constant and continuous reading, which is very helpful in substantiating what might otherwise have been chalked up to an active imagination.

Instinct – Yes, instinct. Humankind has the innate ability to sense when something is dangerous, out of the ordinary, or just not quite right. Undoubtedly remnant of a very early survival tool, gut-level reactions have been responsible for averting disastrous outcomes and saving lives in numbers too great to calculate. Everyone knows someone who is alive today simply because "their gut told them to...." It is this same extrasensory perception that becomes useful in feeling the presence of higher levels of energy conducive to hauntings and apparitions.

What Are We Looking For, Exactly?

Good question. As paranormal investigators, it is our job to pinpoint the source of any alleged paranormal activity, even if that activity turns out to be the 5 a.m. subway train rattling your pictures off the wall, or an insufferable woodpecker trying to burrow through the aluminum flashing on your roof. The tools and techniques employed are done so for the purpose of ruling out all other possibilities, leaving you with only the unexplainable. The caveat to this method is that it really does nothing to completely disprove paranormal activity. Investigators can find perfectly scientific explanations to account for just about any activity, leaving a beleaguered homeowner feeling hopeless and crazy. That is why it is very important to strike a balance between reasonable explanation and grasping at scientific straws. If the client is describing a pounding on his upstairs closet door that is hard enough to crumble the plaster on the walls, it probably isn't the cat scratching at the back door...get the idea? The foundation of any paranormal investigation is built upon evidence gathered in the following ways:

Temperature changes – As mentioned, the thermometer will be used to gauge the amount and frequency of temperature fluctuations. This data would not be a strong enough indicator to use on its own, so it is intended to validate the data collected through the other instruments. It is quite common to experience extreme drops in temperature with haunting and apparition activity, but when those fluctuations are noted, it is important to comb the surrounding area for other possible causes, i.e. poorly sealed refrigerator, cracked window, etc.

Electromagnetic energy – Almost any piece of electronic equipment will give an EMF reading if in close proximity to the detector. The readings we are most interested in are the sudden spikes that occur out of nowhere and cannot be otherwise duplicated. If I am standing next to the stereo surround sound, I would expect the device to give a higher reading, but if I am standing in the middle of a formal dining room with nothing more than a table and chairs, I would have to work a little harder to explain the sudden elevation in energy. If an unusual reading is obtained, it is important to note whether or not the point of energy is stationary or if it is moving around the room. If the building has multiple levels, it should be documented what is immediately above and below the spot in question. And lastly, are you able to reasonably duplicate that reading in the same spot in the room? If the reading cannot be duplicated, it must be noted as unexplainable and would therefore support the possibility of paranormal activity.

Photographic anomalies – There is probably no other topic amongst the paranormal crowd that sparks as much controversy as the..."ghost photos." The truth of the matter is that they are very difficult to capture, and are equally difficult to explain scientifically. In an investigation where two hundred photos are taken, there may be five or six that warrant any further scrutiny. The most important first step in capturing any worthwhile photographic evidence is to have a keen grasp of your camera. You must really familiarize yourself with all of the settings, and know which settings are most appropriate for an indoor investigation. The quality of the image can be affected by inappropriate film speed setting, bad flash setting, or the general spasticity of the photographer. Also remember this: if the photo is blurry, it's useless. Nothing will kill the credibility of a paranormal investigator faster than insisting that every double exposure, glass reflection, or camera strap is a "great capture." Make sure the camera strap is wound tightly around your wrist, and if you have long hair, pull it back. Give the area a white glove test to check for levels of dust, and make note of any air conditioning vents or ceiling fans. Also, be sure to check your light levels, as low lighting can cause shadows that can be mistaken for anomalies. Now you are ready to start taking photos. Once you have completed your photography, you will want to go through every photo with a fine-tooth comb. Evidence can appear in many forms including white mist (assuming, of course, this is a non-smoking establishment), isolated streaks or spheres of light, apparitions, and orbs. Make sure you scour the entire photo, including reflective surfaces. It is not unheard of to find very compelling photographic evidence in photo frames, mirrors, or un-powered television screens; just make certain that the area in question is completely free of tampering or corporeal influence.

Orbs – If you ask ten different investigators to give you their opinion about orbs, you will probably get ten variations of the same answer, depending on which paranormal television shows they watch. Most everyone seems to be jumping onto the "orbs are just dust" bandwagon, probably because it is not as fantastic as capturing film evidence of a chair moving across an attic floor or a fuzzily defined cloaked figure gliding aimlessly through a rundown corridor. Here is the final word: orbs can be just as valid and compelling as any other photographic evidence, but discretion is important. If you have a photograph taken during a windstorm at a softball game, those orbs you see are probably NOT dear departed Aunt Mildred coming for a visit. If you do everything in your power to investigate and secure the area PRIOR to taking the photos, then you can rest assured that your evidence is clean and credible.

Electronic voice phenomena – This is the term used to describe sounds that are recorded during an investigation, but are inaudible to the human ear. Generally, a handheld digital recorder is carried around throughout the investigation to record the goings on, and is played back later to see if any unexplainable noises are found. The other method of capturing EVP involves asking a series of questions such as "Who are you?" or "Why are you here?" and pausing between each of them in the hope of capturing the answers on the recorder. This method is really best used in as quiet an environment as possible. Chances are, if you are investigating a noisy restaurant, the constant din of conversation and activity would certainly drown out any ghostly voices. This, along with orbs, is hotly debated among paranormal researchers. It may be difficult to convince people who were not present when a recording was captured of its authenticity. Take this with a grain of salt. If you are studying paranormal research for your own personal edification, then the opinions (and they are just that) of skeptics should not interfere with your experience. That being said, it is extremely important to scrutinize all evidence and search for other possible causes before jumping to conclusions.

Instinct – This is the tool that provides "sensitivity" to the sensitives. Contrary to what some may say, everyone is equipped with at least a basic sixth sense. This is the feeling you get in the center of your stomach, just under your ribcage, that sends the message that things aren't what they seem. This is the same sensitivity that tells people to take a different route to work, or to wait for the next flight, or not to send the kids back to the new babysitter. When you walk into a building for the first time, and you feel the very core of your being tighten up, that is the gut-level reaction that is letting you know that there is something that warrants investigating. Call it a hunch, but I bet you've all had that feeling a time or two, but shrugged it off as ridiculous. When heeded, gut reactions are an indispensable tool in avoiding any manner of personal and professional derailment. As with any skill, practice makes perfect. Not everyone is born with a high level of sensitivity, but the ability can be honed. Neither is everyone born with a beautiful singing voice, but most people can train their voice over time. That is not to say that everyone will sing professionally, but everyone is born with the equipment and the basic ability to make a sound that approximates singing. Similarly, everyone is born with the capacity for gut-level reactions, but most people will have to learn to recognize these by paying close attention to them and separating them from other feelings that can cloud judgment.

The Different Types of Activity...

Before moving any further, we need to take a moment to make some distinctions. Not all activity is the same and not all phenomena equal the same activity. While nothing in the paranormal is solid, incontrovertible fact, there are three distinct types of activity that have been observed consistently by investigators. These are apparitions, hauntings, and poltergeists. As far as science goes, these are the commonly held classifications of activity.

Apparition – Generally speaking, an apparition is what most people think of when they think of a "ghost." This is literally the spirit of a dead person hanging around a place for whatever reason. When seen, they are usually a white or black shadow, more like a silhouette than a distinct figure. The classic image of a floating white sheet likely comes from the apparition's tendency to be more of a shape, and less a distinct human figure. Usually, an apparition appears in the peripheral vision and seems to interact with some amount of intelligence.

Haunting – The next type of activity is a haunting. This can be a bit confusing if only because the term is used colloquially to describe something a ghost does in a place, but in this case it is technically the name of a different sort of activity altogether. In this case, a haunting refers to an event recorded in time, playing over and over again. The idea is that something happened, usually traumatic, in a place and the event imprinted itself on the area and proceeds to replay over and over again, not dissimilar to a videotape repeating on loop. Another source of confusion regarding hauntings is that they often include human figures doing things, and these figures are mistaken for apparitions. The difference, however, is that the figures in a haunting are not sentient in any way. They will repeat the same actions over and over again and cannot interact with people or their environment. An easy way to distinguish an apparition from a haunting is that the figures in a haunting will usually be wearing clothing or manipulating objects. A lantern or a denim jacket do not have souls and therefore have no place on an apparition. So if you see some guy in overalls with a butcher knife coming at you, it's no big deal...it's just an image burned into that place. Unless, of course, it really is a guy in overalls with a butcher knife. In any case, we leave that for you to distinguish for yourself, and we certainly wish you the best of luck if it does turn out to be the latter of those choices.

Poltergeist – This third type of activity is often misunderstood. Poltergeist is translated from German as "noisy spirit," and is characterized by the movement or disappearance of objects. This is a very sensational form of activity in which doors are opened and closed, windows rattle, objects are hurled across the room, and bookcases fall over. Whenever things are moved or manipulated, that is a poltergeist. Here's the catch: this isn't a ghost at all. Again, nothing is proven or set in stone, but the consensus is that poltergeist activity is caused by unconscious psychokinetic energy stemming from a human source. Psychokinesis is the ability to move or manipulate objects with a person's mind. In this case, the person is doing it without knowing it, usually in response to stress.

It should be noted that none of these types of activity are mutually exclusive, and can actually all happen at the same time. They are distinct phenomena, but they can certainly occur simultaneously. Sometimes the stress of an apparition or a haunting can actually cause poltergeist activity, for example.

Now...all of that being said, we are not going to spend any time trying to prove or disprove any of this. Among those investigators who study the paranormal as scientifically as possible, these are the accepted classifications. We make them a part of our more casual study only to emphasize that there are a lot of people out there with crazy ideas about what a ghost is or what a ghost does. From motion picture references of talking pig heads to statues that come to life, a fair amount of silliness gets tossed around out there. Just because we are a casual study does not mean we are going to play fast and loose with the science.

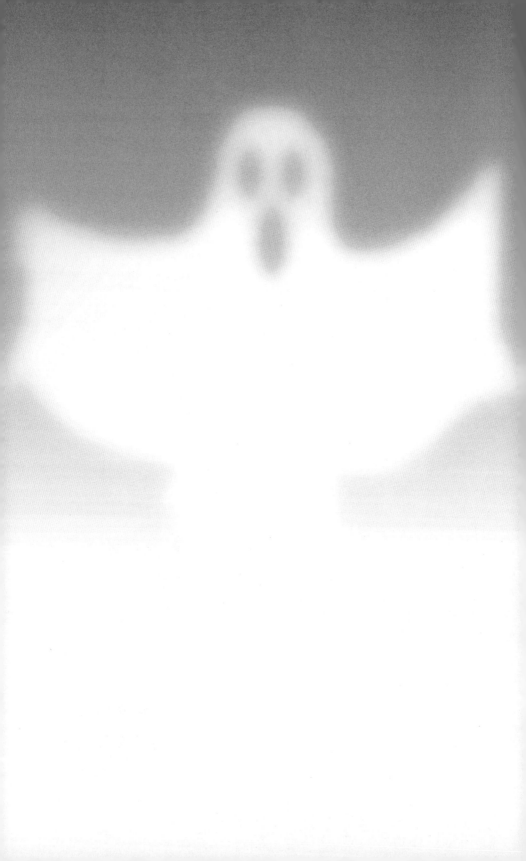

Paranormal Investigator vs. Ghost-hunter ?

The difference between the two? In a word, nothing. The realm of the paranormal has become, in recent years, the newest, hottest topic of interest to hit the airwaves. Television and movies have been focusing more and more on the technical aspects of investigating, leaving behind the out-dated notions of gooey white ectoplasm and floating bed linens. While it can be argued that the upsurge in interest is a result of the media attention, the truth is that ghost-hunters have been around for centuries. Only recently have advances in technology allowed paranormal investigators to postulate new theories regarding the cause and composition of ghosts and hauntings, and this has led to a bit of a division between the two groups. Prior to the advent of political correctness, anyone with a passing fancy in the paranormal would have been referred to as a ghost-hunter. A ghost-hunter is someone who, by widely held belief, goes stomping through graveyards at midnight, telling worrisome tales of phantom soldiers and disembodied voices. Traditionally, they have also had the misfortune of being labeled as anything from eccentric to certifiably insane, and the validity of their claims has been regarded with impatience and disbelief, except to other ghost-hunters.

Nowadays, the more preferred term is paranormal investigator because it denotes a tad more credibility, but in all honesty there is nothing incorrect or bad about either term. The difference between the two groups results from the level of formality in investigative protocol and technique. Paranormal investigators use uniform terminology and established techniques (and fancier, more expensive equipment), while ghost-hunters get their sea legs with more informal means of investigating. I have seen many groups that refer to themselves as paranormal investigators while simultaneously insisting that they are both different from and better than ghost-hunters. This is nothing more than a display of insecurity from a less-than-knowledgeable group and a shady attempt to discredit their peers. They seem to have forgotten that yesterday's ghost-hunters paved the way for today's paranormal investigators, and everyone has to begin somewhere. In this business, that somewhere is generally in the middle of a graveyard at midnight.

Common Misconceptions...

Admit it. You've seen all the television shows about ghosts and you have come to a pretty swift conclusion about exactly how a paranormal investigator looks and acts. We have also watched those shows, most often through the space between our fingers because our heads are buried in our hands from total exasperation, with the same combination of attraction and repulsion usually reserved for train wrecks and family court reality shows. This has led us to our own set of conclusions about paranormal investigators. Particularly, "It certainly is NO WONDER that people think we are insane!" Since our goal is to educate and encourage new investigators, we feel it incumbent upon us to dispel some rather widely held misconceptions about paranormal investigators and set the record straight.

• *Sensitive does not equal psychic*. It is very hard to promote credibility in a line of work where your main competition professes to possess some magical powers exclusive only to their group, even going as far as making up fancy titles to describe these mystical abilities and to impress the uninformed masses. The industry has uniform terminology for a reason. Creating a new term to describe a not-so-new ability is akin to calling a gas station attendant a "petroleum transfer technician." Yes, there are some people in this world that have an honest-to-goodness ability to see dead people and it has been documented. It is exceedingly rare. However, everyone has the ability to sense, at some level, the energy fluctuations frequently found when paranormal activity is present. Some people may feel it as a gnawing at their solar plexus, others may get flashes of images to which they have no tangible connection, or some may just feel the hair on the back of their neck stand up. All of those are very real and should be noted. As far as psychics go, I will apply the old adage, "if it seems too good to be true, it probably is."

• *We are real people with real lives*. We make really great meatloaf, we go to our kids' track meets, and we cry at sad movies. We clip coupons, never pay retail, and become infuriated at bad customer service. We are different in no way from the rest of society, and we make no claims of having special powers attainable only by birthright or incantation. We are the real deal, my friend...no smoke, no mirrors.

• *We do not all have mullets and wear trenchcoats.* Who are these people and why do they get all the airtime? It isn't so much the actual combination of mullet and trenchcoat that is so off-putting, but rather the caliber of the investigator that tends to choose this as his uniform. I am sure plenty of highly educated individuals from all walks of life have had, at one time or another, either a trenchcoat or a mullet or both. They may have even worn feathers clipped in their hair, or a pith helmet. The point is you wouldn't get away with wearing that to the office, so why would you try to pull it off during a professional investigation? Presentation is everything, and perception is reality. Bottom line.

• *We do not worship a dark under-lord, sleep in caskets, or sacrifice small animals.* Many people in this vast and varied world of ours carry around these insulting notions that anyone with even a passing interest in the field of parapsychology is a heartless barbarian who has sold their soul and are doomed to burn for all eternity. Please do not confuse our reference to the existence of these individuals as dignifying that notion with a response. I do think it is funny to imagine the whole lot of them one day wondering, "Why is it so hot in here, and where did this enormous hand basket come from?"

• *We do not wear flowing capes or carry crystal wands.* Okay, out of the entire group of us, I was probably the only one who EVER wore a flowing cape or carried a wand, but I stopped doing that when I was about seven. If you want to spend a gazillion dollars to have your palm read by some bejeweled charlatan, please be our guest. Just know this: cold reading is something that "psychics" go to school to learn. It is nothing more than reading the body language of the subject and responding with broad, sweeping guesses. This is not dissimilar to the deductive reasoning used by Sherlock Holmes, for example; only his was used specifically for the purpose of solving crimes. More information is then gleaned from the reaction of the subject and the whole process becomes this wicked circle of chicanery. It may be FUN to do that, but it is NOT a legitimate, research-oriented branch of paranormal investigation.

• *We don't believe that every building is haunted, or that everyone tells the truth.* Everyone loves to share their scary experiences, or common ghostly lore. Sadly, there are those out there that make a business out of charging you a king's ransom to tell you that your house or business is haunted by sub-humanoid crab people, and when that pocket is empty, they reach into your other one and charge you to "cleanse" your establishment of these poor, lost souls. This is a business that runs on the honor system. Anyone who violates that brings shame to the rest of us.

• *Never, ever pay to have, or take part in, an investigation.* Legitimate investigators will never charge for an investigation. It is our privilege to investigate, and any good investigator will take the time to decide if a claim even warrants further investigation. There are situations that would indicate the possibility of reimbursement or cost-sharing for certain expenses, such as gas (if the investigation is a considerable distance), but even that is on a limited basis. The point of the exercise is to gather data and potential evidence, not to bilk unsuspecting and frightened people out of their money and their sanity. If any paranormal group has a price list, do not contact them. You will only be serving to line their pockets and you will be given nothing tangible in return. Similarly, do not pay to participate in an investigation. There are many groups that are looking for reliable members that do not have any kind of fee involved. They are happy to share experiences with like-minded individuals and only value the input and skills that you bring to the table. Even during the course of researching this book did we have the misfortune of encountering one well-known establishment that decided to start charging three hundred dollars for the opportunity to stage an investigation. Although they are well within their rights to charge any price they deem fair to use the facilities, they are clearly only in it for the money — not the research. Places like this one have received so much hyper-exposure in books and on television that they are now able to turn paranormal investigating into a lucrative side business. Our advice: find another place to investigate. You will undoubtedly be able to see their paranormal activity in a heavily rotated, syndicated rerun at some point.

Ghost-hunting Etiquette...

Because being a paranormal investigator leaves one open to lots of subjective character assessment, it is of the utmost importance to exercise the highest level of professionalism and etiquette when dealing with potential clients. You never get a second chance to make a first impression, but you will get plenty of chances to relive the horror of making an ass of yourself because you were too busy being impressed with your own importance to remember these commandments of paranormal investigation:

No trespassing – This certainly seems obvious, but many would-be investigators have been stopped in their tracks, handcuffed, photographed, and fingerprinted by the local authorities, and deposited where the only spirits they are able to experience are those from the shared hip flask of their cellmate, Bubba, in the county jail. If you are planning to visit and to share information about the establishment you are investigating, or even to post it on your website, then obtaining permission from a property owner is strongly encouraged. We do not possess degrees in any manner of legal study, but logic would dictate that you would have already made arrangements with and received permission from the property owner, and any group of paranormal investigators worth its salt obtains a signed release form before snapping their first photograph.

No drinking or drugs – Again, common sense should prevail here. I can state without hesitation that it is never okay to arrive at an investigation under the influence of any mind-altering substance, prescription or otherwise. Any paranormal investigation should be given the same consideration that you would give to your employer. If someone has trusted you to enter their home or business, do not take advantage of that particularly vulnerable position by showing up for the investigation reeking of patchouli and cheap liquor. Just say no.

No smoking – Smoking during an investigation can cause equipment malfunction when you lose your grasp on that "ultra slim" digital camera while trying to light your cigarette, sending the camera smashing to the ground and shattering it into eight gazillion useless pieces. Also, the smoke from a cigarette can cause unclear photographic imagery, cause messy, yellow grease to build up on the equipment, and make all of the rest of the investigators cough. Never smoke during an investigation — no ifs, ands, or "butts."

No reckless disregard for clients, other investigators, or their property – I cannot overstate the importance of being professional at all times during an investigation. Certainly, there will be times when a bit of humor and levity can be interjected, but at no time should you use profanity towards a client or a member of your team, and at no time shall you engage in activities that will cause damage to the reputation and/or belongings of a client or a team member.

Say "please" and "thank you," and remember the golden rule –
Presumably, your mother did not raise you in a barn. Behave accordingly.

Write these rules of etiquette down, tattoo them to the inside of your forearm, or chisel them into a stone tablet — whatever it takes to remind yourself that paranormal investigation is a serious, albeit esoteric, study of unexplained phenomena. To make light of the sometimes terrifying misfortune of your clientele will only serve to destroy your credibility and the credibility of paranormal investigation in general.

How to Use This Book ?

O kay, great, so you have all this information, but how do you use it? Because the aim of the book is to allow inexperienced individuals the opportunity to conduct their own casual investigations, we've split the location listings into sections. Each location will include a history and general information section — which will include the information regarding the reported activity — and also a section devoted to the results of our walk-throughs. There will also be contact information and directions included at the beginning of each section so that you may contact the establishment and make plans for your own investigation. We have also ranked the locations by intensity and frequency of activity. This will allow you to decide exactly how freaked out you are willing to get, and it will also allow you to gradually work your way into the next location.

The history and general information section is precisely what it sounds like. We give you the background of the place, when it was built, who interacted with it and any other information that may be miscellaneous but no less interesting or important. Obviously, following that line, this section will also detail whatever activity has been reported in the past, including firsthand accounts when available and information from the proprietors of the establishment, as well as local lore. Generally, we are only going to include those stories and reports that have been reported many times or come from credible witnesses. Also, we reserve the right to omit any stories that are unmitigated poppycock. This line of business puts a person in the unique, and sometimes unfortunate, position of hearing numerous accounts of activity and strange goings on. Often times, and perhaps much more than one would care for, you will have to navigate through and decipher the impossible ramblings of the easily frightened and enormously mistaken.

Our walk-through notes will detail what we did when we arrived at the location based on the methodologies discussed previously. Since each location includes our experiences during the investigation, the walk-through portions will be written individually and from our own unique perspectives. The walk-throughs may contain similar accounts of a particular experience, but it will serve as a guideline and basis for comparison for the next group. Again, our methods are modified and much less scientific or formal than your average professional team, but this is a book for beginners and the scientific aspects are something that you will want to work into, if at all. If you are looking to do this for fun, our methods work just fine. If you are looking for a more serious pursuit, we provide a good foundation upon which you can build solid scientific study by adding statistics and more controlled conditions.

If you do choose to go to the next level in scientific investigation, you will find yourself needing to get more access than many places provide the average traveler, and that requires a bit of reputation or legitimacy. Starting out with the relative baby steps provided here will help build that, as long as you conduct yourself with respect and professionalism. If you choose to instead act like a jackass, we cannot help you nor are we responsible for your foolishness.

Since our focus is solidly on the beginner, however, the sections are arranged in such a way that the beginner can find paranormal-friendly locations interested in having the would-be ghost-hunter come through for a look around and conduct a small scale investigation. The history sections will give you all you need to get started and let you know what you are getting into in terms of amenities, and indeed what locations may interest you. We recommend you go to the location and record your findings before returning to the book to find out the details surrounding the reported activity. This will enable you to compare your impressions and experiences to those reported in the past. Our walk-throughs will further provide comparison of reported activity as well as provide a model to follow if you are unsure of how to proceed. Of course, if you just want to read about the places, activity, and our experiences all in one go, that is fine as well. If you read all the way through, bear in mind you will taint yourself for your own investigation if that is your aim.

Again, it cannot be overstated that whenever conducting investigations, you must always be professional and respectful. You may be paying to stay in or visit a place but that doesn't give you the right to act however you'd like. It is hard enough to carve out some credibility in this field without having to deal with the bad behavior of those unacquainted with the acceptable practices of paranormal investigation. The locations in this book are all places that are happy to have you and are generally willing to talk to you about their activity. Bad experiences will erase that goodwill, and can harm the efforts of those who come after you. I have talked to some people who have had such bad experiences with poorly behaved crazy-merchants (who claimed to be ghost-hunters) that they are unwilling to deal with groups unless they have some legitimate backing. Others have turned to charging exorbitant fees for any ghost-hunting group. Sure, greed plays a factor in that equation, but all the same, the bad apples in this case really can spoil the bunch. So, to close out that point, just follow the golden rule and be respectful and you won't have any problems.

SECTION TWO:
HERE'S WHERE TO GO

Bisbee

The Bisbee Inn / Hotel La More

www.bisbeeinn.com
45 OK Street
P.O. Box 1855, Bisbee, AZ 85603
(888) 432-5131

Hours of Operation: Contact hotel directly regarding hotel hours. The lobby is not staffed round the clock.

Directions: From I-10, take exit 303 to merge onto AZ-80/I-10-BL toward Benson/Douglas. Continuing on AZ-80, take a left to stay on same road. Turn left at West Boulevard. Turn right at Commerce Street. Sharp left at Brewery Avenue, turning right to stay on Brewery. Turn right at OK Street. Curbside parking is available. As with Jerome, park your car and leave it there. Almost everything in Bisbee is accessible on foot and the roads are narrow and confusing.

Intensity of paranormal activity: Moderate

The town of Bisbee is located in the southern part of Arizona. Built originally to facilitate the thriving mining population, the town is now filled with antique stores, trendy cafés, and art museums. It is only befitting that this town be described as its own work of art. Layered on the backdrop of undulating red and green hills, the town is carved from concrete and woven together with iron and steel, and delicately beaded with the delightful mélange of free-spirited residents and travelers.

Overlooking Brewery Gulch is the very modest and unassuming Bisbee Inn. Although the land upon which the Bisbee Inn was constructed was acquired as part of the Gadsden Purchase, the actual hotel was not built until 1916. The hotel appears largely unchanged from its original architecture and is furnished with accessories that pay careful homage to its heyday. Formerly known as the Hotel La More (named after one of its earliest proprietors, Kate La More), ownership of this hotel has passed through many hands over the past century, and as of this writing, the torch of the Bisbee Inn is being lovingly carried by Moses and Brena Mercer.

The Ghosts...

There are several ghosts that are believed to be in residence at the Bisbee Inn, although little is known about their origin. The first ghost, Abigail, appears to visitors as a young lady with long blond hair and a flowing white gown. One resident of

Bisbee allegedly had a run-in with Abigail as a small child. As the story goes, he was playing on the hillside behind the hotel when Abigail appeared to him, chasing him away from the spot where he'd been playing. Once a safe distance away, the boy turned back to see that Abigail had disappeared and the spot where he was playing had been the site of a massive rockslide. Had Abigail not intervened, the outcome would have certainly been unpleasant.

Joining Abigail in her ghostly goings on are another lady spirit named Michelle, a tall man who appears wearing a bowler hat, and a cat — seen mostly by children — who makes his home in Room 23.

Katie's Journal...

We arrived late in the afternoon and settled into Room 5. Its location towards the back of the hotel was adjacent to the common areas, making it a perfect location to base the investigation. We spent the first few hours just waiting for everyone to retire to their rooms. Understandably, for most people, staying in a haunted hotel is quite a novelty and invites open and frequent discussions among the guests and staff as to the exact nature of the haunting. Because this is counterproductive to a "clean" investigation, we watched several hours of British sitcoms to drown out the loud discussion from the common areas. When the guests had vacated the area, we began our walk-through. We made several sweeps of the downstairs area and one very thorough sweep of the upstairs. A comparison of notes was fairly unremarkable, although we did both have strong sensations in the kitchen area and the upstairs near the fire exit. Particularly, the sensation that we both reported in the kitchen was that of someone standing right behind us. I turned around several times fully expecting to see some luminous figure, but, alas, it was not to be...at least not at that point.

After a couple of hours of sitting and waiting and monitoring EMF, we felt that the next logical step was to commence the sleeping portion of the investigation, partly because we had collected sufficient information from the walk-through, and partly because we were both beginning to nod off in the lounge area. This time, we were fully prepared with our dream journals. I fell asleep fairly quickly, which surprised me. Normally, I spend so much time wondering if I will wake up and see a dark shadowy figure next to my bed that I rarely actually fall asleep long enough to find out. Although falling asleep was easy, I certainly did not stay asleep for very long...

The first time I was awakened, it was by the sensation of something touching my face. My first thought was, "Oh GOD, there is a spider in my bed!", but after a moment I realized that it was not the feeling of eight legs dancing across my face, but rather the wispy light touch of someone trying to delicately tickle it. It happened enough times that I woke up scratching my face. I made note of it, but was not necessarily convinced it was anything paranormal. I didn't think of it again until the next morning when Patrick reported the exact same sensation.

The second time I woke up was a little different. This time, I could not breathe. I felt as though something was pressing on my chest, and I could not draw enough breath into my lungs to offset the feeling that I was suffocating. Obviously, I was NOT suffocating, but the feeling was intense enough to make me wake Patrick up and tell him that I could not breathe. After several minutes, the feeling abated enough for me to fall back to sleep.

Before I describe what happened the next time I woke up, I want to make some clarifications. As a paranormal investigator, I do have an interest in anything that is outside of the normal boundaries of psychology or science. It pretty much goes along with the territory. However, there are two things that I don't particularly care to experience; the first one is demonic entities. If it growls, scratches, or smells of sulphur, my advice is to contact a gastroenterologist or an ordained priest. The second thing is astral projection. If you are reading this book, I make the assumption that you have at least a general knowledge of most topics relating to parapsychology. If that is not the case, let me briefly explain. Astral projection is the process by which many practitioners believe your soul is able to leave your body and travel hither and thither and anywhere your heart desires. Most people experience astral projection and don't even realize what is happening. Some people can actually cause this to happen at will, but most people have the experience in their sleep and chalk it up to unusually vivid flying dreams. The feelings that accompany this are generally in the arena of a loud buzzing sound in one's ears, an extremely tingly feeling encompassing the entire body, and finally the sensation of floating upwards.

That being said, I can now count myself among those who have had a Bisbee astral projection experience, although I can also say that I am in *NO* hurry to repeat it. The third and final time I woke up, I became aware that I was experiencing the aforementioned floating sensation. I was also aware that I was engaged in some sort of struggle...although it is still unclear to me what I was struggling against. Nevertheless, I found myself flailing about in a state of being half-in and half-out of my body. I was sitting up in the bed, quite aware and displeased that it was not my physical body but rather my astral body. I began to panic and I looked over at Patrick, who was still asleep, and began yelling his name at the top of my lungs. Of course, he could not hear me, and I furiously began waving my hands to try and get his attention, still yelling his name. After several futile seconds of waving my hands, I became aware of a glowing ball of red light that was centered between our beds. I could see the light flicker through my fingers as I frantically motioned to Patrick. Still not able to wake him, I turned to the nightstand and tried to knock something onto the floor, and felt myself screaming at him out of sheer terror, and as I screamed his name I heard a woman's voice screaming his name after me, only her tone was a mocking tone as if to indicate that he could not hear me. Frankly, that pissed me off enough to muster every ounce of energy I could to force myself to snap out of it and wake up as my normal, complete self. My heart was racing faster than if I had just run the Boston Marathon, and my hands were shaking so badly that I could not turn on the light. I immediately grabbed my journal and wrote it all down, careful not to exclude one single detail.

When Patrick opened his sleepy little eyes to see what my ruckus was about, I sternly informed him that I was done sleeping and that the light would remain on for the rest of the night. I let him know that I would be happy to let him read my extensive notes as soon as he was ready. He tentatively replied, "O...K...", and then went back to sleep — just like a guy.

Unfortunately, we had to leave before anyone was manning the front desk, so we weren't able to compare notes with anyone, but we were able to read some recent entries from other guests, including another paranormal group, that mentioned some of the same hits that we experienced in the kitchen and in the upstairs area. I even noticed that one guest had a vivid dream of waking up in the hallway, just outside of another room in the hotel. I certainly do not wish to dissuade anyone from staying at the Bisbee Inn. It is quaint and comfortable, and everyone's experiences are going to be different. I will say that I believe wholeheartedly that there is paranormal activity present in the hotel, and I would further say that it is easily one of my most profound paranormal experiences ever.

I enthusiastically give the Bisbee Inn two disembodied astral thumbs up!

Patrick's Journal...

Bisbee is a winding and hilly affair in which everything is within walking distance — but that walking is going to be done mostly up staircases and across rickety bridges, and the streets can be a bit confusing. For this reason, I parked in the first lot I could find that was reasonably close to the signs for the Bisbee Inn, also known as the Hotel La More, and walked the rest of the way. That sort of thing is fine if the hotel in question is not at the top of a hill, which, unfortunately, is exactly where this one was located.

The Bisbee Inn is an unassuming structure nestled between the Hot Licks Saloon and an old apartment building. It has a very pleasant and welcoming look and indeed after carrying baggage and equipment up the hill, the benches were something of a godsend. We checked in and made our way to Room 5, a cozy double room at the end of the hallway on the first floor and right next to the hotel's sitting room and dining area.

These back portions seem to have at one time been an outdoor patio as the ceiling of the dining and sitting rooms are vaulted up to the second floor. The second floor itself seems to have some exterior windows facing into the open space, lending further credence to the idea that this was the product of a renovation. It also meant that sound carried a bit from upstairs to the downstairs. As is often the case, the hotel was full to capacity for the night and there was understandable bustle both upstairs and down. Katie and I, upon returning from an uphill romp around Bisbee, had to sequester ourselves in our room, which was thankfully quiet with the door closed, to avoid the chatter regarding the hauntings. When you are attempting a blind study, this sort of thing can be a problem — given that people tend to talk openly and excitedly about the haunted place in which they are staying. We countered this by watching television on my laptop until the activity quieted.

Once the hubbub had more or less subsided, Katie and I did our walk-through. The area isn't huge so we made several circuits of the downstairs area as well as making our way up perhaps the creakiest staircase outside of a Laurel and Hardy vehicle. Honestly, aside from the sense of not being alone at the emergency exit, the upstairs didn't do much for me. It could have been the almost dead silence up there aside from our footsteps that was off-putting, but I didn't get much from the upstairs and wanted very much to be back on the first floor. Sure, my aversion to the second floor could conceivably be interpreted as something paranormal, but if the goal is to look for confounds and more likely explanations, I think that Occam's Razor points pretty directly at my own sheepishness about making too much noise up there.

I felt I was on more solid ground on the first floor, and it was here that I felt the most activity. Of particular interest was the kitchen area. I consistently felt a strong presence in this room. Indeed, the whole of the back of the hotel — from the kitchen to the sitting room — seemed to be pretty happening. I spent a decent amount of time in the sitting area doing just that. It seemed like this was the place to be, and I tried out different positions in the room and eventually caught sight of someone walking out of the dining room and into the kitchen. I followed quickly and found no one at all. It was startling and also gave me motivation to help myself to a granola bar.

Eventually we retreated back to the room for sleeping, and I found myself in the bed next to the window. Looking out the window, I found myself peering at the asphalt outside and realizing that because the hotel is built upon a hill, the ground came right up to the bottom of the window and my bed was effectively below it. Pushing away thoughts of someone walking up to the window and letting themselves in to do to us as they please, I went to sleep.

Now, when sleeping over, dreams can be just as powerful as any other experience one may encounter in an investigation, and Bisbee is known for particularly vivid ones in its haunted locations. My dreams — the two that I documented — were both very disturbing. Both dealt with me sitting in that particular room while being told to kill myself. The first was by hanging as I dreamt I was preparing the rope while a female voice instructed me on what to do. Before shuddering awake, I was dreaming of writing a note. The second dream was far less vivid and much more circumspect, but was again dealing with my impending suicide in the hotel.

Amidst these horrible dreams, which I assure the reader are not in any way motivated by any desire of my own to carry out such actions, I also found myself waking up and scratching my face as if something was touching it. I didn't think much of this beyond hoping desperately it wasn't some manner of spider crawling on me until Katie told me the next day that she too had awakened to the same feeling and the same scratching. She was having some issues sleeping and eventually announced she was keeping the light on and would not be going back to sleep. Of course, since I was driving, I went back to sleep for a short while, eventually finding that sleep would elude me. We left before the manager came in for the day, but did read some of the accounts of other people's stay in the guest log...some described [the paranormal] activity in the hotel. A few described similar experiences to the ones we had and others described hearing footsteps down the halls upstairs, and I couldn't help but wince at the idea that they had simply heard us on our investigation.

While our particular night was not peaceful and pleasant for us, that is not to say there is anything bad or evil going on in the hotel. Sure, having dreams about killing yourself is not all puppy dogs and ice cream, but aside from those dreams, I didn't feel any thing bad or evil in the place. Indeed when walking around it was very pleasant and I didn't feel anything negative. Everyone experiences things differently, so our individual experiences should not color anyone's impressions of the place. When you consider the story of the apparition shooing a boy away from death at the hands of a rockslide, I think you'll find that my dreams can't be taken as proof positive that the hotel is trying to kill its guests. It's pleasant and nice and fairly active and a deserving stop on any ghost tour. Bisbee is a pretty haunted place in general, and the Bisbee Inn fits right in.

THE OLIVER HOUSE
26 Sowle
P.O. Box 1681, Bisbee, AZ 85603
(520) 432-1900

Hours of Operation: Guests are welcome to come and go at their convenience. Please contact the Oliver House for more information.

Directions: Same directions to Bisbee as to the Bisbee Inn. The Oliver House can be a bit tricky to find as it blends in to the scenery and must be accessed by a footbridge. As a point of reference, the house is located next to the old high school. Parking is available relatively close to the house. Park and stay put.

Intensity of paranormal activity: Moderate to high

Standing just below the old Bisbee High School, the Oliver House is something of a hidden treasure in Bisbee. It is somewhat difficult to find, but it is definitely worth the search as it is largely considered one of the most haunted places in town...if not the state. Built in 1909 by Edith Oliver, the two-story bed and breakfast has seen its share of tragedy. The House, which has been everything from a mining office to a boarding house in its ninety-eight years of operation, has claimed the lives of twenty-seven people. These deaths were not all peaceful either. The body count includes not only an unsolved murder but a mass murder as well.

For a place with such a death toll, it is odd that there is not more information regarding the history and goings on at the place. Miners primarily occupied the house and, in some extreme cases, there were apparently some rowdy ones. This would include the miner who found his wife in bed with another man and who proceeded to shoot the both of them and several other innocents in a room-to-room spree before turning his weapon on himself. In 1920, there was the shooting of Nat Anderson at the top of the stairs. Anderson did not survive and the gunman was never found. It is speculated that the killing was retaliation for unpaid gambling debt, but the supposition was clearly not enough to lead the authorities to the shooter.

The Ghosts...

Not surprisingly, with all the death and mayhem in the boarding house's past, the Oliver House has seen quite its share of paranormal activity. The reported activity runs the gamut of disturbances:

Footsteps can be heard at night, doors and window shutters open of their own volition, furniture moves around the room, and even spectral sounds of water dripping down nonexistent pipes.

The activity doesn't stop with all that either — it is also not uncommon to feel marked drops in temperature in certain spots in different rooms and figures have been seen walking the halls at night....

While most of the activity occurs upstairs, the ground floor does see its share of action. In limited cases, the rooms involved in the mass murder have provoked a sense of disorientation and dizziness in some visitors. It's much less frequent than the goings on upstairs, but it has happened from time to time.

Unique of Room G, a former management office, people have experienced *Terry*, a manager of the Oliver House who passed away and seems to like to introduce herself in people's dreams. If one were to look for a room in the place that has the most activity, G, or Quince's Room as it is now called, is definitely the one. Not only is it Terry's old office, but it's also right next to the stairs and subsequently right next to the site of Nat Anderson's murder. Unsurprisingly, this area at the top of the stairs tends to provoke feelings of dizziness...as well as feelings of not being alone.

A little more on the odd side of the paranormal experience, the Oliver House is also somewhat notorious for astral projection. This occurs when guests are asleep and often feel like they are walking on the streets of Bisbee in nothing but their bedclothes and bare feet. Certainly this is a bit more on the sketchy side of the spectrum of experience, but when dozens of people report the same thing, there may be something there.

The Oliver House clearly enjoys a wide range of activity and is a good bet for activity. It has gotten a good deal of attention from paranormal groups throughout the years and is consistently turning out results. The Oliver House is definitely worth the effort it takes to find it.

Katie's Journal...

Where do I begin with the Oliver House? This place is so over-the-top brimming with activity that I am practically exhausted just from this one investigation, but it's a good tired. We began our investigation later in the evening and we had the unique good fortune of being, quite literally, the only guests booked for the night, and were given free reign to the entire upstairs area. This is a paranormal investigator's absolute perfect world scenario.

Initially, we walked through the rooms individually, strictly taking notes and making diagrams of any thoughts, impressions, or feelings. We were able to take as long as we needed in each of the rooms. We were staying in the rather notorious Room G, which is now referred to as Quince's Quarters, so this room would be used for the overnight portion of the investigation. For the sake of brevity, I will refer to the rooms by their letter, rather than their proper names.

Just to clarify the process on this particular investigation: because he had been there twice before and was completely informed on the nature of the hauntings, Patrick served as a "control" on this investigation. Mikal took a few notes of his own, in addition to taking the photos so that we would allow ourselves the greatest opportunity for hits.

I began my walk-through in Room I. A bright and cheerful room with green walls and floral bedspreads, it seemed likely to be rather innocuous, but as I sat down on one of its beds, I suddenly felt as though someone was standing in the corner of the room, watching me. This feeling did not frighten me, but it was very intense. I made note of the exact position in the room that drew my attention, then I moved next door to Room K.

Entering Room K...felt like a sandbag to the stomach. The feeling of a presence was so intense that I almost expected it to materialize right in front of me. I am fairly certain that if it had, I would have required immediate resuscitation. I was very drawn to this room, but I also felt very much like running in the opposite direction. Even Mikal, who is as skeptical as they come, reported seeing a shadow moving around the room. I felt particularly drawn towards the wooden door on the opposite side of the room. If the feeling of a presence in that room could have been likened to an explosion, the feeling at the wooden door would have been "THE EPICENTER." Although I could have stayed in Room K all night, I moseyed along to Room M.

The first thing I noticed about Room M was the busy wallpaper, and I wondered how anyone would notice any paranormal activity with such a busy backdrop. I honestly felt no particular sense of activity in this room — until I heard the wooden floor on the opposite side of the room make a creaking noise. As we have said repeatedly during the course of our investigations, nothing should be ignored. I later asked Patrick to take an EMF reading in that part of the room, and, to no one's surprise, the reading was extraordinarily high.

An orb watches intently at the Oliver House.

Across the hall from M is Room L. My initial feeling of this room is that it seemed very hazy and foggy. I blinked my eyes several times thinking they were just very dry, but the cloudiness remained. Aside from the visual disturbance, I had no other feelings about this room. Room H, on the other hand, is a completely different story....

Room H is, as you might guess, next door to L. As with Room K, I immediately felt as though someone were standing across the room, sizing me up. Interestingly, this room is diagonally across the hall from Room K, and these are the two rooms in which I had the most intense sensations during the first part of the walk-through. There are two other rooms on the second floor, but I had no sense of activity in the remaining rooms and chose to focus my investigating efforts on the rooms that held the greatest sense of paranormal activity.

After taking what we felt to be a sufficient amount of notes on the general feeling in each of the rooms, we got out the equipment and circled the upstairs a second time. The EMF was definitely working overtime, and we were getting very high readings in the hallway and in rooms H and K. I was very excited since the readings we were getting fully supported many of the impressions that I had noted, and also the idea that the Oliver House was haunted.

Of course, no well-rounded paranormal investigation would be complete without at least one or two good cases of the heebie-jeebies. Case number one: while passing through the hallway, I was walking with my hands crossed behind me since I was not carrying any of the equipment at that time. As I made another pass between rooms H and K, I distinctly felt a very light sweeping touch to the back of my left arm. I immediately looked at the back of my arm and did that, "What's on me? Get it off!", dance that you might do if you feel something touch you, but then I realized there was nothing there that could have caused that sensation. Everyone else was investigating the other rooms and I was alone.

Case number two actually happened during the overnight portion. I awoke in the middle of the night because I am a terribly light sleeper on these investigations. I was completely still in the bed, and everyone else was sound asleep and motionless. I became aware of the sensation that something was pulling the sheets, as though someone were climbing into the bed and the pressure caused the sheets to tighten around my leg. The sensation was slight, and I moved my leg a bit to make it stop. When I was once again still, the sensation returned that something was pulling the sheet. This happened three times in a row before I finally just closed my eyes and fell back to sleep. I later found out that this is quite common in Room G.

When morning broke, we had a chance to compare notes from the previous night's walk through — and I was floored to find that we had nailed a couple of the same things. As I had suspected, Room K was a hot spot for everyone during the walk-through, even my twelve-year-old son (who is just beginning to learn the investigative ropes). We all concurred that there was definitely a feeling of a strong presence in that room and some of the photographic evidence seems to support that as well. We also captured some fairly compelling photographic evidence across the hall in Room H. Even compared to some of the entries left in the downstairs guestbook, we had amazingly similar results.

Honestly, I don't think that I have been to a more active location since the Jerome Grand, which we discuss later in the book. Fortunately, the activity is limited to the second floor, which is a lot less ground to cover. In terms of any type of paranormal investigation, I would have to say that the Oliver House is an exceptional place to visit, whether you are just starting out or if you are a seasoned professional. You are practically guaranteed to experience some manner of paranormal activity, and the convenience of not having to walk through four expansive floors of an historic hotel make it a mandatory assignment in the school of ghost-hunting.

~~~~~~~~~~~~~~~~~~~~~~~~~~~~

Patrick's Journal...

The best way to find this unassuming structure is to look up at the old high school, a dominant building on a prominent hill, and then look straight down from there. Even when you've made your way to the parking lot, you are still looking at a walk past a few houses and across a bridge that goes over a very moat-like drainage tunnel.

I've been to the Oliver House three times now over the past ten years; once on an official investigation with the Pima College group and twice on my own. Given this was my third trip, I was in more control on the walk-through...although I did have some fresh experiences this time around.

Upon arriving at the Oliver House, we found we were the only people staying in the place that night and we had full run of it. This was excellent as it gave us an opportunity to do a full walk-through of all the upstairs rooms, something we have not had in previous investigations for the book. The room we chose was the somewhat infamous Room G, a former business office turned guest room that has the reputation of being the most active in the B&B.

The first time I visited the Oliver House I stayed in Room G as well. At that time there was no shower, two beds, and I didn't really have much of an investigative methodology in place. I just wanted to check it out. I had completed Bill Everist's parapsychology class at the time, but it was prior to any experience with an official investigation, and I was playing it much more by ear than we do now, even with our current casual methods.

Not much happened while I was awake, and I left the place that first time somewhat disappointed. It wasn't until I talked with Bill the next week about my stay that I realized how important dream journals were to the investigation process. I wouldn't even have told him about this had he not asked, but as it turns out, it was the most significant part of that stay. In my dream I was sleeping in Room G and a woman in a white nightgown came up to me and said hello and put out her hand to shake it. I was taking her hand as she said her name was Terry, and it suddenly occurred to me that no women in white nightgowns should be standing at my bedside. I woke up with a scream and found myself sitting upright all the way across the bed. Apparently, I had gone from a dead sleep on my side to screaming and flying across the bed. Upon telling Bill this, he smiled and told me that I was the third person to have experienced that dream. Evidently the former Oliver House manager, now deceased, likes to introduce herself to men staying in her former office.

As far as my second visit to the house goes, I am not at liberty to discuss any findings or data as it was not my investigation, but I can say that while sleeping in what was Room M, which is now called Morning Glory, I experienced an astral projection. Astral projection, as Katie mentioned in her journal for the Bisbee Inn, is essentially believed to be when one leaves their body in spirit form and wanders around the ethereal plane. This may sound fairly odd in the broad light of day and to someone who has not had the experience, but then the platypus is a pretty odd thing, too, and that is real.

Whether experienced alone or as part of a dream, the astral projection experience is mostly something done on an unconscious level, the perception of which is reported with great consistency. As with anything in the paranormal field, I cannot definitively prove it's real, but I can describe the experience as I have felt it. The short of it is that you feel weightless and can fly about, moving through objects and unable to communicate or manipulate things. You're sort of like what someone might think of as a ghost moving about as you please until you come back around to your body. Personally, I hate when it happens and I don't like the feeling of this state.

Since Bisbee seems to have a fairly high instance of unconscious astral projection, I will mention that during my second stay at the Oliver House I found myself tooling around town in an astral form. Can I prove to you it wasn't just a dream or I am not just crazy? No, but plenty of other people have had the same experience. At the very least, I have shared another dream with people I don't know.

Upon arriving at the Oliver House on this last visit, I found that Room G, now named Quince's Quarters, had a new shower and only one bed. I found myself sleeping on a couch the size of a steamer trunk, and while lying awake throughout the night, I found myself wishing it had at least been a pullout. Katie's son's discovery as we were packing up the next morning that it was, in fact, a pull-out did very little to improve my mood.

After a tasty meal at the local Santiago's Mexican Restaurant, we made our way back to the Oliver House and started our walk-through. Since we had the whole floor, we made floor plans of all the rooms and headed into them one at a time.

When you walk out of Room G, you are right there at the top of the stairs. My first impressions — while possibly colored by the knowledge I already had of the place — were that of a presence right there at the top. Moving throughout the floor I found that rooms N, K, and I were giving off a vibe. Particularly, I found myself dizzy and tentative and, in every instance, not alone. Rooms I and K felt especially active and I found them somewhat difficult to stay in.

The hallway itself creeped me out, and I often felt followed. I also felt chills on my back and the back of my arms as I walked it. Because we were doing this one at a time, I can rule out anyone actually being behind me.

Following our initial walk-through, we went back for another pass with our equipment. This pass found some interesting verifications with the EMF detector. We got heavy readings in the hall around the spots in which both Katie and I felt something behind us, but the readings were not consistent in the way something mundane like electrical wiring would be. The readings were here and there and seemed to follow us.

While I didn't feel anything in Room M on the walk-through, Katie had heard the creaking of floorboards in this room, and needle-burying EMF readings in the spot added to her suspicions about the room.

Again, given I have been to the Oliver House in the past, my impressions here on the last trip have to be taken with at least a small grain of salt. It's entirely possible that my experiences were the product of my knowledge of the place and its activity. However, the fact that a great deal of my hits matched up exactly with Katie's demonstrates what we want it to show when trying to do this sort of investigation. It's about replicating the reported behavior. When one of the central criticisms of the paranormal and its study is the general inability to recreate results in a laboratory or test environment, the repeating of experiences is of course helpful to the cause.

It's not proof positive of course, but it's compelling once you get enough consistency.

If there is one thing the Oliver House has, it is consistency. The reported activity is pretty consistent in both frequency and mode. This means when you stay upstairs at the Oliver House you are getting as close to a sure thing as you are likely to find investigating the paranormal. The Oliver House definitely earns its reputation as one of the most haunted places in Arizona, and no trip through Bisbee is complete without a stay there.

Douglas

The Gadsden Hotel

www.hotelgadsden.com

1046 G Avenue, Douglas, AZ 85607

(520) 364-4481

Hours of Operation: Hotel lobby is open and staffed twenty-four hours a day. Please contact the hotel for information regarding the restaurants located on premises.

Directions: From I-10, take exit 303 to merge onto AZ-80/I-10-BL toward Benson/Douglas. Continue to follow AZ-80, turning left to stay on it. At traffic circle, take third exit onto AZ-80 South. Follow to Gadsden. Parking is available curbside.

Intensity of paranormal activity: Low to moderate

Located in Douglas, the Gadsden Hotel is another stunning example of an establishment where past meets present. Originally built in 1907, the hotel, whose name refers to the Gadsden Purchase, was a popular destination among miners, ranchers, and businessmen long before Arizona became a state.

The hotel was constructed with such attention to detail that even by today's standards the lobby alone would be considered a priceless work of art. The focal point of the lobby is a massive marble staircase that encompasses one quarter of the space, joining both halves of the first floor and flowing downward like a luminous river of white gold. Rising above the staircase is a genuine Tiffany stained glass mural that runs a full forty-two feet across both arms of the massive staircase, while four gigantic marble pillars provide both structural integrity and eye candy to the rest of the lobby. The top of each pillar is adorned with 14K leaf gold, a decorative touch that was quite expensive in 1907 and would surely be beyond fiscal reason in today's architecture.

The Gadsden's famous marble staircase.

Understandably, this grand and ornate structure has not only been an attraction for visiting guests, but also with Tinseltown. Many full-length features have been filmed inside of this stately dame, most notably "The Life and Times of Judge Roy Bean." Since opening its doors, the Gadsden has been host to many dignitaries and celebrities, and legend even tells of Pancho Villa riding his horse up the expansive staircase, chipping the marble of one step and forever embedding his presence within the hotel.

The Ghosts...

Many yarns have been spun regarding the nature of the hauntings at the Gadsden. The most widely held belief is that there are at least three ghosts wandering the halls of the hotel, disturbing guests and staff, and making their presence known. The stories originate from a love triangle — a cowboy named Jonathan and a soldier named Jacinto, vying for the attention of their beloved Annie. Not much more is known about this threesome, but many reports of activity certainly include sightings of a cowboy and of a dark shadowy figure.

Katie's Journal...

I think the overall tone for the Gadsden was set when, as we entered Douglas, the theme from the movie, "Ghostbusters," came on the radio. We actually laughed out loud. Not long after the song ended, we arrived at the hotel and unloaded our equipment from the hearse – err – car and checked in. Not unlike the other vintage hotels we have visited, the lobby of the Gadsden made me feel like I should be wearing bright red lipstick, dressed in my finest vintage flowing gown, complete with the sultry Veronica Lake wave covering my right eye. Fortunately, good sense stepped in and reminded me that I was there for a very different, if not diametrically opposing reason, and we made our way up the striking marble staircase to our room on the next floor.

Honestly, with as many people as there were milling about the lobby, I wondered if it would even be a remote possibility to manage any sort of a decent walk-through. We waited for a few hours, but the lobby stayed busy. In retrospect, a Saturday night in one of the most popular social spots in Douglas, Arizona may not have been the best day to attempt an investigation. Nevertheless, we forged ahead.

We made our way up the next flight of stairs to the second floor (even though we had to climb the stairs to our room, it was still technically on the first floor). Once the large metal door closed behind us, it seemed like a completely different hotel. The noise from the lobby was completely silenced, and there was definitely a creepiness about the upper floors that was not apparent in the lobby. Perhaps the constant din of activity provides a security blanket for those who wish to ignore the laundry list of reported paranormal occurrences.

We began walking through the second floor, working our way up to the fourth floor. As I walked through the second floor, I noticed that I was registering very high EMF spikes that were not attributable to anything else that I could find, and they were very random. At one point, I found myself at the end of a very long hallway, and I began to feel like I was not alone. Honestly, it was not the strongest sensation I have ever had, but it did make me take notice.

The next stop was the third floor. As I reached the top of the staircase leading to this floor, I turned and looked up the stairs towards the fourth floor. I immediately had the sense that someone was standing on the staircase watching me, and that sensation was validated by another EMF spike. This was really the only time in the hotel that I felt that really intense, this-place-freaks-me-out sensation that I have had in all of the other locations. That does not mean that the hotel is not every bit as active as the other locations...it just means that in the finite amount of time that we spent at the Gadsden, I did not find myself in any sort of chilling, spine-tingling situation.

As we walked through the third floor, I continued to get the sensation that I was being followed, and I had the image in my head of an older man in a white hospital gown. I made note of it because I thought it was odd, and it may have been because the green and white tile floor lends itself to the feeling of being in an old hospital. The feeling was particularly strong on one side of the hotel and occurred again in the laundry area. This laundry area had a small water closet that was being remodeled — and it was receiving another very high EMF reading.

The fourth floor was uneventful save for a few spots of feeling lightheaded, but that could have just as easily been attributed to the fact that I just hoofed it up four flights of stairs. I was actually feeling a little disappointed when Patrick and I went to the front desk to ask about gaining access to the legendary basement. We had both heard through the grapevine that the basement was supposedly the scene of an unusually high level of activity, although we had always been careful not to hear anymore than that. We asked the front desk clerk if there was any chance of going to the basement and, as I suspected, we were not allowed access. When we explained that we had heard that all of the activity was in the basement, she said,

"Who told you that? There are ghosts all over the hotel. Have you been to room 333?"

"Room 333?" I repeated. She explained that everyone who comes to the Gadsden looking for ghosts wants to stay in Room 333 because of all of the alleged activity. Armed with this new piece of information, we made our way back up to the third floor and found Room 333. I immediately compared it to my notes and found that the same location where I had the sense of being followed was just outside of Room 333. Finally, a hit! Patrick also noted that he had a similar sense in precisely the same location. I was glad that we could end the walk-through with a little bit of evidence, albeit a very little.

We turned in for the evening and slept like babies. No noises, no sleep disturbances. The following morning we returned to the front desk to make a second attempt at gaining access to the basement, but once again we were not able. We were like two ships passing in the night with the hotel manager, and it just did not pan out. On a positive note, the hotel keeps an ongoing journal of paranormal activity that is accessible to anyone who wants to read its "ghost book." Even though we had a pretty light experience, it appears we may be in the minority. Based on the journal entries written by previous guests and dating back many years, there is an abundance of activity. Many guests report seeing a cowboy appear in their room at night, several have experienced inexplicable disturbances such as telephones that ring with no one on the other end and lights that turn themselves on and off, and some even report hearing the sounds of disembodied voices from their room into the hallway...only to find an empty room. One desk clerk even refuses to use the downstairs ladies' room out of sheer fright.

Although we had only a small amount of activity, the Gadsden Hotel is definitely one that any paranormal investigator should put to the test. Not only do they have numerous reports of activity, the staff is very open to paranormal investigations and it is a perfect place to gain experience.

Patrick's Journal...

Unless taking a wrong turn on the way back from the fast food restaurant district, the Gadsden Hotel is easily the most recognizable landmark Douglas has to offer. Looming above the town, it's a blocky white behemoth with a red neon sign like a beacon in the night. Looking at the building from the outside it doesn't look like a historically significant landmark but rather a warehouse or book repository. Entering the hotel, however, your assessment of the place is immediately amended.

The lobby of the building is a grand and sweeping affair, filled with pillars and couches and floors of marble. There is a grand staircase at one end and an equally impressive front desk at the other. The lobby is truly a beautiful sight. There is a restaurant, gift shop, and very old-fashioned elevator that must be controlled by an operator. There is even a stuffed mountain lion hunted and killed by the hotel's manager.

Impressed by the lobby, we checked in and received our key to our first-floor room. Hopping into what proved to be an exceptionally speedy elevator, we made our way quickly to Room 130. The first floor is unique to the rest of the hotel as the rooms circle around a wide-open area above the lobby. This first floor seemed almost an extension of the lobby as tables and chairs line the railing around the opening where you can sit and socialize with other guests or use your laptop with the free wi-fi. The lobby and first floor have a very unique ambiance and is quite nice.

It should be noted that while the Gadsden is listed in the National Registry of Historic Places, the hundred-year old building has received no government restoration money. Because of this the rooms can be somewhat rugged. The benefit of staying at the Gadsden will be to experience a historical place and perhaps some paranormal activity. In a general sense, modern hotels don't often come equipped with ghosts, so some of the more lavish conveniences must be forfeited for the overall experience.

After an ill-fated trip for fast food, we let the lobby activity die down to a dull roar and began our walk-through. Katie and Mikal started their walk-through while I hung out on the balcony a bit longer as I wanted to give the place more time to quiet down. It was a busy Saturday, so I waited for quite a while. I headed up to the fourth floor and while we couldn't go into any other rooms aside from our own, we did a circuit of the halls. The layout of the upper floors is essentially an "H" pattern and staircases allow access at either end of the building.

On the fourth floor, I didn't really get too much aside from a few scattered feelings of butterflies or not being alone. It was easy enough to draw floorplan maps once I got a feel of the layout, and I marked the places I felt something. I didn't bring the video camera along for this trip if only because every time I watch the videotape I can see myself almost falling down the stairs or toppling over various end tables. At any rate, the fourth floor seemed pretty quiet.

Moving down to the third floor was a whole different ball game. Now, the Gadsden didn't leave me with terribly strong impressions; indeed, it was one of the quietest places I've been to. That being said, the third floor did give me the strongest impressions in the place. Walking down the left arm of the H, if the stairs were your starting point, I found myself feeling distinctly followed. This wasn't a passive sense of someone lurking in the distance; it was very immediate and aggressive in its persistence. I felt very much like someone was right there behind me — and it was fairly off-putting. Of course, looking back, there was no one there.

After making note of the location of my impressions, I went back down to the main hallway and found the laundry room. Entering the room I was struck again with a strong sense of not being alone. This feeling intensified as I poked my head into the bathroom, which was in the process of being remodeled. Katie got some fairly high EMF from the area, so I am fairly confident that there was some action there.

The rest of the walk-through was uneventful until we got back down to the first floor and into the Kopper Room, which seemed to be some manner of meeting hall. Perhaps it was the odd and unpleasant smell in the room, but I found myself dizzy and a bit shaky. After wandering around in there for a bit we ended the walk-through portion and headed off to bed.

As has been mentioned previously, an overnight investigation is a bit different in that you have to keep stock of your dreams and anything else that might happen in the night. In the case of the Gadsden this would include nothing but a good night's sleep. While the bed wasn't the most comfortable I have ever slept in, the sleep I received was perhaps the best I have had the whole time I have been investigating.

Upon waking up and having a somewhat rugged shower, we went to the front desk to see if we could gain access to the basement, which we had heard was the primary location for activity. As it turned out, only the hotel manager can accompany people down there and like a bad slapstick comedy, we kept missing each other. Despite this, we found out that the basement was not the only place that had activity but the entire hotel was reportedly active, most notably Room 333. I wish we would have known this initially so we could have booked that room, but such is fate of the blind study.

Now knowing of at least one hot spot we made our way up to the third floor once again to take a look and see where Room 333 fell in terms of our impressions. As luck would have it, both of us experienced the feelings of being followed right in front of that room. Looking at the door, someone had carved 666 under the room number, and while the belief that the activity in the room is the work of the devil is certainly very suspect, it did go a little further in affirming the room's level of activity.

As with anywhere, the Gadsden has its pluses and minuses and just because we didn't get a whole lot of notable results does not mean that not much goes on. The hotel keeps ghost logs that guests can use to write down their experiences and given that these are two volumes' worth, plenty of people have experienced plenty of things. The stay will be a mixed bag for sure, but you have a good shot at some activity at the Gadsden, especially if you book Room 333 or any room on the third floor. One request, however, if you contribute to the "ghost book": please mind your handwriting so that your experiences can be read. Some of the scrawl in the journals more closely resembles Sanskrit than English. It's for posterity so be kind and keep handwriting in mind.

GLOBE

NOFTSGER HILL INN BED AND BREAKFAST

www.noftsgerhillinn.com

425 North Street, Globe, AZ 85501

(928) 425-2260

(877) 780-2479

Hours of Operation: Guests are welcome to come and go at their convenience. Please contact the Noftsger Hill Inn for more information.

Directions: Take Highway 60 to Broad Street and follow signs. Building is at the top of a relatively steep hill with narrow streets. Ample parking is available on premises.

Intensity of paranormal activity: High

Located in the historic mining town of Globe, the Noftsger Hill Inn Bed and Breakfast offers fantastic scenery and accommodations to curious travelers from all over Arizona. Originally built in 1907, the building started life as the North Globe Schoolhouse.

The name was eventually changed to Noftsger Hill School in honor of the man who owned the hill upon which the school was located. During its tenure, hundreds of students passed through its doors — most notably, former Arizona Governor Rose Mofford. The school eventually closed its doors in 1981.

Now owned and operated by Dom and Rosalie Ayala, the Noftsger Hill Bed and Breakfast has managed to perfectly capture the history of the building. The rooms are huge and filled with antiques — right down to the claw foot tub in the bathroom. The parlor is a stunning place for guests to relax and enjoy the magnificent attention to detail the Ayalas have achieved in the renovation. The walls are lined with vintage photos of the school, and there are even some original schoolhouse relics adorning the building. Staying at the Noftsger Hill Bed and Breakfast actually *FEELS* like staying in an old schoolhouse, except you have the finest amenities of any bed and breakfast that I have ever been to. The integrity of the schoolhouse is never compromised, and its transition to bed and breakfast is seamless.

The Ghosts...

Based on history, there is really no specific traumatic incident that could pinpoint the reason for the activity that occurs at the inn. Many groups have investigated the building, and some even claim to know the identities of the deceased. While we don't necessarily believe that anyone knows who is haunting the place, we do believe that it *IS* haunted. Many guests report hearing the sounds of children laughing and giggling. Also quite common are the heavy sounds of footsteps.

An orb – apparently late for class – hovers in the parlor of the Noftsger Hill Inn. The staircase reportedly sees consistent activity.

Katie's Journal...

I must admit that, prior to my visit to Noftsger Hill Inn Bed and Breakfast, I was beginning to wonder if I was ever going to have one of those "haunted house" experiences that perhaps only occurs in movies. That question was most definitely answered during our investigation.

We arrived in the evening and were greeted by Rosalie, an extremely friendly and accommodating hostess, and were shown to our room on the first floor. The building immediately impressed me. The view from the outside never betrays its vintage scholastic appearance. The inside has been transformed into a vast and beautiful home away from home for visitors to the inn, and the entire length of both the top and bottom floors of the old schoolhouse are lined with antique furnishings and relics from the school's past, including the two original cement staircases just inside the original front entrance. Both parlors are also filled with games, books, and videos for the enjoyment of the guests, or perhaps more to keep their minds distracted from the ceaseless amount of paranormal activity that occurs. I am telling you, if there were ever the possibility of a Grand Central Station-esque terminal for the loading and unloading of passengers into the afterlife, this is the place — right smack dab at the top of Noftsger Hill in the otherwise uneventful town of Globe, Arizona.

Our room was impressively large and very well-appointed. With two queen beds at one end, and another twin bed and leather sofa at the other, it could have easily accommodated a large group. An inviting sitting area, perfectly arranged for game playing, separated the two ends of the room. We made ourselves at home in our room until around 10:30 p.m., at which time we decided to officially begin the walk-through. Mikal and I had already walked around the building, taking a few establishing photos, and familiarizing ourselves with the common areas. I should have taken it as a sign of things to come when we captured a large, brilliant orb hovering in the center of the downstairs lobby. I was also sure I had seen a white, misty figure — ever so briefly — in the upstairs parlor, but I chalked it up to a light reflection and returned to the room.

For this particular investigation, we opted to leave the voice recorder on a dresser top while we walked through the rest of the house. We turned it on and promptly forgot about it as we began investigating. As with our other investigations, we walked around separately and made note of certain specific impressions. I don't really know exactly what it was about this particular location compared to all the others, but I felt a definite hesitation within myself with each step I took around the building.

In the upstairs parlor, I found myself particularly interested in one of the corners of the wall opposite the staircases. From the moment I entered the floor, I felt so strongly that I was being watched that I actually had the sense that I was trespassing. Whatever was watching us seemed to want us to know that we were treading on its turf. Interestingly, as I stared tentatively into that corner, I looked at the door next to me and could clearly see the outline of the word "PRINCIPAL" etched into the glass, and I suddenly felt like a little kid waiting to be called in to find out what my punishment would be. My gaze continued towards that corner for several minutes until I was distracted by the slight, almost undetectable movement of one of the parlor's rocking chairs. It rocked exactly twice, as if to give me just enough of a warning to stay out of trouble. The other portion of the building that gave me pause was the area downstairs, between the staircases. As I stood there, I felt as though people were gathered on the steps — again, just watching me.

Satisfied that we had collected sufficient impressions, we headed back downstairs to the room. I turned off the voice recorder and we mulled about for a bit until it was time to turn in for the evening. Admittedly, since the whole Bisbee Inn experience, I have found myself a tad more reluctant towards the going-to-sleep portion of the investigation. Nevertheless, I turned out the light and closed my eyes. Evidently, that was exactly the cue the ghosts needed to rev up for the nightly show. No sooner did the lights go out than Mikal said, "Something just sat on my foot!" He quickly snapped a few random photos and, once again, we attempted to sleep.

I guess I must have dozed off briefly, but that didn't last very long. I awoke to find Patrick scrawling aggressively in his dream journal, which made me terribly curious and also even more hesitant to go back to sleep. As I lay in the relative quiet of the room, I suddenly heard the very distinct noise of a large piece of furniture moving swiftly across the wooden floor in the hallway. My heart raced a little with anticipation, and I entertained the thought of peering out the door of our room, but I have seen far too many horror movies showcasing the terrible misfortune for the girl who wanders into harm's way, armed only with myopia and fuzzy nightclothes.

When I was awakened a second time, I hadn't even realized I had been sleeping. I opened my eyes to find Mikal — our resident skeptic — staring at me, probably willing me to wake up, just to tell me:

"I can't sleep in this haunted house."

The voices from the hallway were keeping him awake, as was the jingling of a pet collar (which I had also heard). Important to note: There are no pets that roam freely through the building. The resident cat had been put to bed in the owner's quarters hours before the investigation, and there was absolutely no other evidence of a pet being in the vicinity. Reassuring Mikal that it would be fine, I dozed off for a third time.

The next thing that woke me up was the loud and distinct sound of a heavy, wooden ball rolling across the floor towards my bed. I immediately opened my eyes to investigate, but no sooner did I open my eyes that I felt the familiar whoosh of another out-of-body episode, akin to my aforementioned previous experience, only this time it felt like tiny hands were pulling at my shoulders. I believe my exact thought was, "Oh, *HELL* no!" and forced myself to sit up in bed. I was relieved to see Patrick was also awake and I watched him walk from the side of his bed over to the window (although, in retrospect, I find it noteworthy that even though I *SAW* him walking, I did not *HEAR* him walking, which would have been impossible to miss given that the floor is made from genuine Brazilian squeak wood shipped in directly from Loudtown), but as I reached for my notepad, I heard another whoosh, and I realized that I was still in the middle of the blasted astral projection. With every bit of effort I had, I forced my eyes wide open and this succeeded. I turned on the light and there was Patrick, sound asleep in his bed, who only moments ago was walking around the room...I had no explanation for this and I was certain that I was not dreaming. I grabbed my dream journal and began writing about the rolling ball, and I quite clearly heard the delighted squeal of a mischievous child whose prank had succeeded. Once I heard that, any fear that I had at that moment disappeared, and I just rolled my eyes like I do at my own children.

At this point, the sun was starting to come up and Patrick was awake. Breaching the normal protocol of the official post-investigation discussion, I immediately began grilling him about what he had experienced. He told me that he spent most of the night in that waking sleep state (conducive to astral projection) and that he felt he was walking around the room all night. I told him about my experience, and that I had actually *SEEN* him walking around, but when I snapped out of it, he appeared to be asleep in his bed. The next thing he tells me is that he'd seen some filmy mist hovering over me in the middle of the night.

Okay..."Check please!"

That was all I needed to hear. As far as I am concerned, the building is haunted. Not in a bad way, just in a very active way. We spoke with Rosalie again that morning, and she specifically made mention of some of the things that we had experienced. Other guests have reported hearing the sounds of children and, as luck would have it, we were staying in one of the most active rooms. She also mentioned that a lot of activity gets reported around the staircases, as well.

Compared to the other investigations we have been on, this is absolutely the most full-blown, four-alarm hotspot that I have visited in all of my years of investigating. Not only did the experience of staying at the Noftsger Hill B&B offer a buffet of paranormal activity rarely seen off screen, but also the evidence we collected is, by far, the most compelling. On any investigation, one can easily expect to have a few chills and capture a few orbs. What every professional group hopes to capture are apparitions. One of my most profound impressions on the investigation was the feeling that someone was watching me from the upstairs corner. Upon close inspection of the photos that Mikal had taken, one exterior shot quite clearly shows the image of a young woman wrapped in a shawl, gazing out the window. That window just happens to be in the very same corner that attracted my attention.

An exterior shot of the Noftsger Hill Inn.

A close-up of the window reveals a spectral onlooker.

Also notable is the evidence that was captured on the voice recorder. As I mentioned, we started the recorder and forgot about it while investigating, and it wasn't until we returned home that we had an opportunity to review it. I began listening to the recording and I heard the sounds of us leaving the room. We left the door to our room ajar to minimize the overall noise level and to make accessing the room easier. A few minutes into the recording and well after we left the room, the bathroom door can clearly be heard slamming shut and latching. There was no other noise, no footsteps, no creaking floorboards, and the airflow from the cooler would have naturally kept the bathroom door open unless a stronger, opposing force closed the door. To make the recorded evidence even more interesting, the sound of a lady's voice can be heard a few moments later, drawing a gasp as if shocked by something. As impressed as we were with this jackpot of evidence, we all concurred that we were equally glad that we didn't hear it until after we got home.

To collect this much evidence and to have such a broad spectrum of experience is any paranormal investigator's dream come true, especially for a professional group. Given the rumors that other visiting groups couldn't stand the heat and ran screaming from the kitchen at a full clip in the middle of the night, I find the experience that much more profound. To anyone wishing to investigate the Noftsger Hill Inn for paranormal activity, you will not be disappointed. If your goal is to spend a pleasant and comfortable night at the most beautiful bed and breakfast in Arizona, run by the nicest folks you could ever hope to meet, you will also not be disappointed. Hands down, Noftsger Hill Inn is the best.

Patrick's Journal...

If paranormal investigation is like treasure hunting, the Noftsger Hill Inn Bed and Breakfast would be the equivalent of finding a secret cove of hidden pirate treasure complete with a full scale Spanish galleon and more gold and pearls than could ever be spent. Also Jimmy Hoffa and Amelia Earhart would be perusing the findings about the Kennedy assassination and inventory lists for Area 51. I don't want to foreshadow too much, but this place was as active as Bourbon Street during Mardi Gras.

As with most of the towns we've explored on this tour, the streets of Globe tend to be of the uphill persuasion. Certainly there is quite a bit more real estate on flat ground than Bisbee or Jerome, but there is a good portion on hills. And when I say hills, I don't mean that it has a mild slope; some of the roads get to a point where you expect to be completely vertical at the next turn. Such is the road leading up to the Noftsger.

After a somewhat harrying drive up to the place, during which I couldn't help but wonder how we would explain to someone how our car came to rest in their living room after crashing straight through their roof, we made it to the Bed and Breakfast. From the outside, it looks nice but somewhat nondescript. Its white form is much like any other old school from that time period. After ringing the buzzer and meeting with Rosalie, the owner, we were ushered into the building and found ourselves in an enormously beautiful and well-tended interior. You won't forget it was once a school, but the main floor is filled with antique tables, chairs, and plush sofas all arranged for visiting with other guests and relaxation in general. There is a refrigerator stocked with drinks and a table piled high with board games and cards. Almost every other surface is covered with books of every sort...and this was just the bottom floor. The top floor was similarly tended with the addition of an aquarium and dozens of videotapes available for your viewing pleasure.

The room was enormous. I can't overstate enough how shocked I was by the sheer amount of floor space. Outside of some manner of suite, I have never seen a room so large. It had two queen-sized beds on the far end of the room and a smaller twin bed in a corner across from them. The middle of the room had a circular table surrounded by very comfy chairs. There was also a desk, TV with built-in VCR, and more books adorning the nightstands and tables. The bathroom was spacious and not at all uncomfortable. I mention this if only because the bathrooms have not always been so nice in our travels so this one was a refreshing change. This was easily the nicest room I have encountered in my years of visiting hotels and bed and breakfasts.

We settled in and began our walk-through around 10:30 p.m. Katie and Mikal went out and took pictures on their own a bit before the walk-through and then we all went out together. Before leaving the room, Katie set up the voice recorder and we left the door slightly ajar as we left. I took the video camera along this time as I wanted a visual reference and because, frankly, just being shown around earlier in the day had given me some dizziness and I thought we might catch some evidence.

Nothing really sorted out on the video camera, and aside from some reasonably profound feelings of not being alone at the stairwell and upstairs, I didn't get a huge response from the walk-through. The floorboards of the place are *VERY* creaky and loud so most of the walk-through was spent with me trying to ninja my way around without waking up Rosalie or the other three ladies staying in the place. While we had no complaints, I can't believe I was in any way successful in this endeavor and perhaps had I been walking across live mousetraps in a fire-cracker factory as it caught fire I could have made less noise.

So, armed with that embarrassment and a very unnerving feeling of being watched, I took the camera back into the room after about twenty minutes. Dropping it off I went back out to find Katie and Mikal were returning, having completed their portion. So I got a diet coke, sat by myself in the lobby for a few minutes, and went back in the room.

I couldn't really put my finger on how I felt at this place. Walking around I felt something, but it was different and I couldn't place it at first. I am used to all manner of the willies and hot and cold spots, as well as feeling like I am not alone or being followed, but this was not like that. It was only after a decent amount of reflection and polishing off the leftover Philly Cheese steak from dinner that I realized that it was the feeling of being watched. That is an odd thing to feel and I don't normally get that feeling. Even feeling like someone is standing behind you is a more passive feeling, this was very active...whatever was watching me was very aware that I was there and that was fairly unnerving.

Still, the walk-through was more uneventful than others and I felt a little bit disappointed. After all, this was the place that had made lesser groups flee in terror in the middle of the night so I was sort of bummed that I hadn't had anything terribly profound yet. Such is life though, and I was ready to chalk it up to another trip where things just weren't that active. By and large I find myself somewhat envious of the people who sign the ghost logs detailing these profound overnight experiences, describing phenomena that would be at home at the Cineplex, and all I come home with is a crick in my neck and a lingering terror that maybe I won't be able to get out of the shower before the raising water level overtakes me. But shortly after lying down to sleep, I realized that as the song says, "times-they are a-changin'...."

Before I get into my sleepy-time activity, I want to touch on a couple of points. The first is to again reiterate the importance of dream journals. I hit on this on every one of the overnight walk-throughs if only because these hastily scrawled notes done in the dark can offer up some of your best evidence. Also, you may forget or decide that you didn't really see it or whatever it was wasn't important and thus miss a corroborative piece of evidence. The second is to mention that given the length of time I have been doing this and the fact that I grew up in a haunted house, I don't get scared. Ever. The Jerome Grand is the only place where I have ever felt any real fear before. So this evening was one of firsts for me....

I went to sleep fairly quickly and stayed that way for about two hours, which was nice as it was the only solid block of sleep I would get for the rest of the night. Initially, I was really hot and kicked off all the covers. This was odd because we'd set the A/C to the "wind tunnel" setting and it was nice and cool before I got in bed. So, unfettered by covers I drifted off to sleep and into dreamland.

In this case, dreamland was the room I was staying in during the day, sun shining in the windows, and I was frantically moving about the room throwing equipment out of bags and yelling, "Is this good enough yet?", at the top of my lungs. I got the impression that someone was there with me, someone authoritative and judging me. Whatever it was...it was amused by my frustration, which grew over time. In the dream, all of a sudden I was freezing and I woke up to find that I was indeed very, very cold.

An anomolous light floats past the ceiling fan at the Noftsger Hill Inn.

When I woke up, it didn't feel so much like waking up as shifting from one reality to another. That sounds crazy, I know, but it was much like when you watch a movie and it goes into a flashback and then snaps back to present day. It even had a "whooshing" sound along with it.

The room after the dream seemed quite a bit darker and I felt completely terrified. I looked across at Katie and Mikal in their bed and I could see Katie fairly clearly with her eyes closed, but what I also saw was someone else lying in the same spot as though they were superimposed on one another. It was like a double exposure in a picture, and what's more, it was looking at me. Flipping over to my other side I found that the feeling of being watched was even more prevalent that way. I also realized I really needed to pee.

It should be mentioned that in addition to never being scared, I have never felt like it was a chore to get out of bed and relieve my bladder as opposed to wetting myself in the night. This is fairly standard operating procedure for your average adult without some sort of medical condition. In this case, I found myself in very serious debate. I hadn't been more scared to get out of bed and go to the bathroom since I was six and my mom told me there were alligators circling my bed that would eat me if I got up from a nap.

I eventually decided that the embarrassment of wetting myself was more persuasive than any paranormal fear might ever be, and I padded my way to the bathroom. I say "padded," but setting off dynamite in a mineshaft doesn't make this much noise.

Upon returning I found Katie and Mikal had stirred and were awake, though miraculously not from the noise of me walking ten feet to the bathroom. I scrawled my notes and went back to sleep.

I am not really sure how long that lasted, but if it was more than ten minutes I would be shocked. I was hearing sounds across the way from Katie and Mikal's bed. We've gone on several of these investigations and I know their sounds pretty well by now, and this sounded like a high-pitched voice making noises and giggling. While Mikal has been known to snore a time or two, it never sounds like a little girl giggling or making noises. Trying to be cool, I went back to sleep.

The rest of the night I never got past the hypnogogic state of sleep. This is the stage of sleep prior to REM where you are hovering in and out of consciousness. If a person is prone to sleepwalking or talking in their sleep, this is when it's going to happen. Also, if one is going to unconsciously astral project, now is the time. I can't say for certain if I projected at the Noftsger, but it would certainly explain why waking up felt less like waking from a dream and more like popping back into this reality. The look and general feel of the room seemed consistent with the out-of-body experience, so it's entirely possible.

Whether I astral-projected or not, the dreams I had were recurring ones involving children asking me questions. Granted, I knew this was a school and I could have been projecting expectations into my subconscious as I slept, but these dreams were like none I have ever had before. Aside from that, the extreme feelings of being watched and hearing the sounds and voices around me woke me up constantly during the night.

There was really no good state of being. If I were asleep I'd be woken up soon, and when I was awake, I was genuinely and intensely terrified. I am not really sure what I was scared of because nothing in the room suggested any hostility, but I think it was a natural reaction to the very intense concentration of the unnatural. If I were to guess, it was that intensity that put me off my game and made me want to get the heck out of Dodge.

Being a professional, I did not run screaming from the place at 3 a.m. Morning, however, was a very welcome sight, and I was ready to wrap up and vacate. We did exactly that after speaking with Rosalie, who made us some lovely breakfast burritos and couldn't have been more accommodating. Her stories seemed to confirm some of the things that happened to us and all of us came out of it feeling like it had been the wildest and most active night on the trip.

It's important to understand that while I was scared and freaked out by this place, it wasn't a bad or evil place at all. I never really felt threatened or in danger in any way, it's just *VERY* active. If your aim is to have a paranormal experience that you've seen in the movies, this is the place to go. I can never guarantee activity in a place, but our experiences were highly profound, and I can't say that if someone else told me these stories...I wouldn't be at least a little dubious about their veracity. So, it's with that in mind that I suggest you go to the Noftsger and have your own experience. Even if there is no activity, it's a very cool place and Rosalie is as nice as she could be so you will not be disappointed. Stay in Room 3 and buckle up 'cause you are in for one wild night....

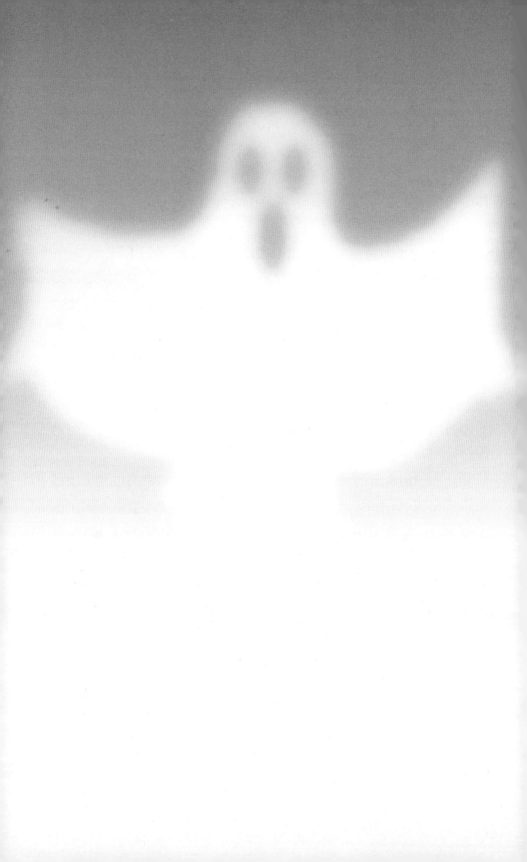

JEROME

THE CONNOR HOTEL

164 Main Street
P.O. Box 1177, Jerome, AZ 86331
(928) 634-5006
(800) 523-3554
www.connorhotel.com

Hours of Operation: As with any hotel, guests have access round the clock. Please contact the hotel for gift shop hours.

Directions: From I-17 North, Take exit 287 for AZ-260 toward AZ-89A/Cottonwood/Payson. Turn left at AZ-260/AZ-279/ Finnie Flat Road and continue to follow AZ-260/AZ-279. Turn left at South Main Street and again at AZ-89-ALT. Make another left to stay on AZ-89-ALT. Make a slight left at Lower Gulch Road/Lower Gulch Crossing and continue to follow Lower Gulch Road. Turn right at Upper Gulch Road. Turn left at AZ-89-ALT. Continue on Hull Avenue. Turn left at Jerome Avenue. Turn right at AZ-89-ALT North. Parking is available curbside and directly across the street from the hotel.

Everything in Jerome is accessible on foot, and navigating the narrow roads can be quite harrowing. Once you find a decent parking space, leave the car and walk everywhere.

Intensity of paranormal activity: Low to moderate

B uilt in 1898, the Connor Hotel is situated squarely in the heart of Jerome. The architectural offspring of David Connor, this hotel has a colorful past that has seen it rise to the height of luxury and fall into flophouse disrepair. The hotel has burned to the ground and been rebuilt two times, and with its recent renovation and upgrades, is now the darling of the town. Even the bricks that were used to rebuild the hotel were chiseled out of the very ground that surrounds the township and were fired in nearby Cottonwood.

Its original heyday dates back to the late 1800s when it was considered one of the most popular destinations in the west. It provided such amenities as bus transportation to and from the train station and the newest luxury — electricity. Each room was equipped with a call button so that the needs of each guest could be met promptly and completely. Sadly, the luxurious status of the hotel could only last as long as the mining money flowed freely, and as that industry waned, so did the popularity of the hotel. By 1931, the hotel closed its doors and the only portion of the building that continued to operate were the shops downstairs. Soon, business was just barely enough to allow the merchants to earn a meager living.

The 1950s brought with it the official closing of the mines, and Jerome soon became an honest-to-goodness ghost town. For the next decade, residents made every effort to capitalize on the tourism that came along with such a kitschy distinction. The town saw an upsurge of popularity by 1960 when the town became a mecca for the newly emerging hippie counter-culture, and this popularity continued into the 1970s. The popularity of the hotel also began to rise, but the attraction was less about the luxury and amenities and more about its proximity to the town's numerous taverns and watering holes. Due to an absence of required fire safety features and also to inadequate electrical wiring, the hotel closed once more in 1980. It again sat vacant for two more decades until the current owners took on the remarkable renovation that has resulted in the beautifully restored jewel that it remains today.

The Ghosts...

Even during the many closings of the hotel, it seems that there are residents that never vacated the premises. Numerous sightings have been reported of a dark-haired woman wearing a red dress whose image is depicted in a painting that hangs above the bar in the adjacent Spirit Room. One hotel guest has even reported feeling a decidedly amorous unseen visitor snuggle up next to him in bed — an experience that sent him running from his room to his vehicle, where he remained for the rest of his stay.

Although she may be the most documented ghost occupying the Connor Hotel, she is by no means the only ghost. Staff members have also reported seeing a man in the basement, dressed in clothing from the late 1800s, who is believed to be the ghost of David Connor himself. Those who have seen him report that he seems to be watching them, undoubtedly making sure that the hotel is being held to his exacting standards. Based on our experience at the Connor Hotel, I am certain that he is not disappointed.

Katie's Journal...

The Connor Hotel is located at a tiny but bustling intersection in the center of Jerome. Unlike its more widely known competitor, the Jerome Grand, the Connor Hotel is actually conveniently located in the center of an entirely uphill community. To check in to this perfectly charming hotel, we entered through the gift shop and were immediately greeted by the soft Celtic music that one would expect in such a decidedly Irish establishment. I instantly felt right at home. At check in, we introduced ourselves to Cynthia Mouritsen, who was welcoming guests at the front desk, and were given actual keys on brass key rings — a clear indication of the attention to detail in this wonderful vintage hotel.

When we opened the door to the hotel room, we were amazed at the size of the room. From a traveler's standpoint, you just don't find hotel rooms as spacious as this one, especially in such a non-metropolitan community. Since it was still early in the day, we decided to do a few touristy things before getting to work on the investigation.

At about 9 p.m., we started our walk-through of the upstairs portion of the hotel, taking photos and getting baseline readings. At times, Patrick and I both had the tiniest feeling of butterflies, but really nothing as extreme as we had felt in previous investigations. We felt a little disappointed after the walk-through, but that is the nature of this business. One day you might have a dozen hits; another day...you get zilch. We knew we still had plenty of opportunity for hits during the overnight part of the investigation, so we adjourned to our room. At this point, Patrick and I decided to go for a late night stroll through Jerome...just to see what might materialize. Mikal stayed behind.

The moment we turned the corner away from the hotel, we were instantly on edge. The town that was filled with tourists and activity only a few short hours before was now so still and silent...you could hear a pin drop. As we walked further away from the hotel, it became an endurance test to see how far away we were willing to venture. There was not one living soul around — Jerome quite literally became a ghost town. We got almost all the way to the ruins of the jail, but the darkness made it too difficult to maneuver and the compromise to our safety was not one that either of us was willing to make.

We began to walk back towards the hotel...unable to escape the feeling that we were being silently escorted by any number of unseen pedestrians. Not only does Jerome have an incredibly high concentration of haunted buildings, but also the town itself is said to be haunted. At any time, one might expect to see the image of a long-dead miner strolling alongside modern day visitors — in most cases, each one blithely unaware of the other's existence.

Our return route took us past the burned out remains of the Bartlett Hotel. Once a very luxurious hotel, the charred ruins are now surrounded by a very foreboding wrought iron fence. Under the warm safety of daylight, this hotel is a rather engaging tourist attraction. The Jerome Historical Society has placed numerous receptacles in what would have been the hotel lobby, into which visitors are encouraged to throw coins to help fund the restoration of the building. Take away the tourists and add a combination of impenetrable darkness and deafening silence, and you have the perfect backdrop of a horror movie. You would just need to include a creepy guy in a clown mask and a rusty torture chamber. Perhaps this description is a bit exaggerated, but you get the idea.

We spent a great deal of time wandering around the perimeter of the ruins, pausing frequently to stand in silent awe. Even resting my camera on the iron bars to take a picture made me uneasy. Through the quietness, it was easy to imagine that the building actually had a pulse, and it was equally as easy to imagine the burned hotel pulling me through the bars and swallowing me whole. Not willing to chance it, we returned to the Connor.

We went to sleep, armed with journals within easy reach, ready to record any dreams and impressions we had throughout the night. What we were not prepared for was the difficulty we would have actually staying asleep. We would later discover that this was another example of being so wrapped up in waiting for the big stuff to happen that we almost missed out on perfectly legitimate paranormal activity presenting itself in an utterly forgettable fashion. Falling asleep was relatively simple, but each time I began to drift off I felt as though my throat was tightening and I would find myself gasping awake. Since I am normally plagued by any and every seasonal and regional allergy known to mankind, I chalked it up to having forgotten my trademark over-the-counter twenty-four-hour non-drowsy allergy medication. Each time I woke up, I also noticed that I was about fifteen degrees hotter than the time before. When that happened for the third time, I decided to wake up completely rather than succumb to the inevitable spontaneous combustion. It was a helpful distraction that Patrick was also wide awake at 3 a.m., so we discussed how odd it was that we would both be awakened from sleep because we were burning up...yet the window was open and the actual temperature in the room was somewhere in the 60s. Even Mikal, who is the first one to complain if the temperature climbs up past seventy-four degrees, was bundled up, sleeping like baby.

Patrick had mentioned that once he was awake, he got the sense that someone was walking through the hallway and he felt compelled to look out the peephole. When I looked out the peephole, I immediately had the vision of a woman with a flowing dress leap into my mind. I did not actually see this woman; it was just one of those instant and inexplicable thoughts that are easily dismissed. We decided that since we were already awake and had completed as much of the investigation as we reasonably could have, we would seize the opportunity to do some research about the hauntings. Several search engines yielded very little information, but there were a few references to a "lady in red" that had been reported — even sending one hotel guest running from his room to spend the rest of the night in his car.

Later that morning, at a more respectable time, we ventured to the front desk to see about first-hand accounts. As we approached the desk, Cynthia mentioned that she had already had several other hotel guests report that they experienced some strange goings on in the night. Instantly intrigued, we summoned the nerve to approach one such group of guests to ask about their experiences.

Rebeca Cardenas and her mother, Cecilia, were visiting the Connor Hotel with their family and both reported unexplained occurrences. Cecilia found it especially difficult to sleep because each time she would fall asleep, she became aware of the feeling that something was squeezing her throat and making it difficult for her to breathe. I was very surprised to hear this since I had experienced the exact same thing, but as I mentioned, I had completely dismissed it, citing allergies. In retrospect, I am not sure why I would have categorized that particular sensation as allergies when I have never had such a reaction to my allergies before. In addition, Cecilia also reported the sensation that her bed was shaking, which made for a rather unproductive night of sleep.

Rebeca, not being one to suffer paranormal activity easily, reported sleeping with earplugs to shield her from any manner of creaks and bumps that could be attributed to ghostly activity, but that did not prevent her from having an experience of her own. Just moments before we spoke to her, Rebeca stated that she had been walking along the sidewalk directly in front of the hotel, and the dress of one young lady caught her eye. She described the dress as long and flowing, and the girl as having medium brown hair. She followed her down the street, paying attention to which storefront the girl entered with the hope of getting a better look at the oddly out-of-place dress. When she arrived at the point where the girl had turned from the sidewalk and entered the building, she was surprised to find that it was in fact *NOT* a storefront but a solid wall. Not only did the phantom girl fit the description (almost exactly) of the random image that popped into my head earlier that morning, but the point at which she vanished into thin air is located right next to a placard commemorating "Husbands' Alley" — a passage frequented by well-respected men seeking to engage in not-so-respectable activities — featuring a picture of a young girl in a long, flowing dress.

Right:
Plaque commemorating Husbands' Alley, where Rebeca saw the young lady vanish.

HUSBANDS' ALLEY

WITH JEROME'S ROUGH AND TUMBLE EARLY DAYS CAME THE RED-LIGHT DISTRICT AND PROSTITUTES. MUCH OF THE RED-LIGHT DISTRICT WAS LOCATED ON HULL AVENUE, THE ROAD BELOW MAIN STREET. IN 1913, REFORMERS HELPED PASS AN ORDINANCE RESTRICTING HOUSES OF ILL FAME FROM BEING LOCATED DOWNTOWN. CITIZENS SHOWED THEIR DISDAIN FOR THE LAW BY NAMING THE ALLEYWAY FROM MAIN STREET TO HULL AVENUE "HUSBANDS' ALLEY". RED-LIGHT DISTRICT BUILDINGS ON HULL AVENUE INCLUDED THE CRIBS, A BRICK STRUCTURE THAT NO LONGER EXISTS. THE LADIES JAIL IS STILL CURRENTLY LOCATED ON HULL AVENUE IN THE BOTTOM FLOOR OF THE NEW STATE MOTOR BUILDING.

Picture of two prostitutes in the Crib

FUNDED BY THE JEROME HISTORICAL SOCIETY

Whether this young girl is the one seen in the photo remains to be determined, but what has certainly been established, as far as I am concerned, is that the Connor Hotel definitely has paranormal activity. This hotel is perfect for beginning investigators who want to familiarize themselves with the steps of a walk-through without having to cover a huge amount of square footage. If you happen to have an interest in the paranormal but are still just a bit freaked out at the idea of staying overnight in a haunted building, I would highly recommend the Connor Hotel. The hotel is delightful and the ghosts are as friendly as the staff.

~~~~~~~~~~~~~~~~~~~~~~~~~~

Patrick's Journal...

Jerome, on the whole, is an enormously unique place. For one, you have the fact it is built on the side of a mountain and its streets weave their way up the mountain like a great snake basking in the sun, with buildings built around it. Further, the buildings are all very historical with very few modern-looking structures adorning its hills. The place just teems with history, not to mention bikers and artisans. It has a feel decidedly its own, and walking its streets you get the distinct impression of the weight of that history all around you (as well as the sort of burning in your legs and back that comes with far too much sitting and typing, and not nearly enough hiking and going to the gym.)

Situated snugly in the middle of the upward sprawl, the Connor Hotel occupies the corner of an intersection with a peculiar elegance. The cornermost section of the structure houses the Spirit Room, a bar that features live music and demonstrates the odd duality of a historical ghost town with a bustling tourist trade and local nightlife. The sounds of rock and the artisan-driven commerce blends into itself so completely it becomes exotically normal.

The Connor itself is everything you would want from a historical building. Its atmosphere and decor are appropriately period but pristinely maintained. Feelings of comfort permeate the establishment, and it was difficult to feel ill-at-ease here, even on a ghost-hunt. The room was surprisingly spacious and very well tended. Often in historical places, everything is historical including the furniture and amenities, which tend to translate into sort of shabby and uncomfortable. This was not the case with the Connor and I was immediately impressed by just how nice the room was. The free wi-fi connection was also nice.

Because it was early in the day, we occupied ourselves with checking out the shops around town and eating lunch and eventually dinner. You will find no fast food places in town so the offerings are all privately owned restaurants or grills. The two we stopped at were exceptional, although it should be noted that one tends to pay for quality, so attention should be paid to one's budget.

After the day wore down a bit, we returned to the Connor for our walk-through. Because this is a working hotel with other guests, our walk-through was restricted to the hallway and common areas, so aside from a few butterflies around the stairs, I really didn't feel much. Given some of the results we've had while writing this book, I felt a little let down, but on overnight investigations the walk-throughs are a smaller part of a larger world.

Katie and I decided we wanted to see what Jerome was like after dark and maybe snap some creepy nighttime pictures, so we went out to the street and just sort of wandered about. What had previously been clogged by tourists and travelers earlier in the day gave way to dim streets, deep shadows, and the sound of drum solos drifting out from some of the surrounding bars. Even in the darkened streets, the sounds of various forms of merrymaking carried into the night.

Eventually, we found our way down the mountain to an area much less frolicking with nighttime socialization and inebriation. Our goal was to take some pictures of the old jail that had managed to slide down the mountain but still remained intact. Making our way down there, however, we found it to be completely devoid of streetlights and therefore a sketchy walk. When all that is standing between you and a roll down a mountain is a rusty and loose handrail, you tend to be a little more conservative where you tread in the dark. Aside from the obvious physical risks, I found myself seeing things. I was fairly convinced that I could see shapes moving in the darkness, and the fact that Katie and I had the distinct feeling of a close proximity pursuit did little to shake that assertion.

On our way back we found ourselves in front of the shell of what was once the Bartlett Hotel. The place had enjoyed a rich history in town before it eventually burnt down. As it stands now, there are bars surrounding it and a collection is being taken up by the historical society to restore it. The side of the building facing the main street is hollowed out, leaving only the basement floor, which is littered with eclectic containers into which the passerby can flip coins to aid in the restoration. Around the corner, however, the street slants down and what's left of the front of the building can be seen in the form of burnt out walls into which double doors are set.

We decided to get some pictures of these ruins as they would make for some spooky night vision shots but in doing so both of us started to feel decidedly uneasy. Looking into the darkened hallways through the sets of double doors, you get the distinct impression something is looking back. At one point I put my face close to the bars and felt an almost certain sense that at any time someone could reach through and grab me. We walked down the street along the full length of the building and the feeling mounted even as we came to parts with no outer wall of any kind. The space seemed positively alive in only the deadest sense — and we felt compelled to flee back to the relative safety of the Connor.

Arriving back at the Conner, we made preparations to go to sleep. I bundled up in the covers, leaving the window open to the chilly March air. After only an hour of sleep, I found myself wide awake and sweating. I had thrown off the covers altogether, but I still felt as if I were on fire. After feeling compelled to look out the peephole, I took a trip to the bathroom, which in contrast felt refreshingly cool. I then got on the computer because I couldn't see myself going back to sleep anytime soon with the heat.

About this time, Katie woke up and said she couldn't sleep either due to the heat and difficulty breathing, so we stayed up for a while, talking and comparing notes. After an hour of this, we decided to take another crack at sleep, so we returned to our respective beds and finally found some small amount of rest. Oddly, at this point I was freezing and had to be completely wrapped up in the covers.

When we woke the next morning, we went down to talk to the hotel staff and get the scoop on the place. The lady at the desk told us some stories about having seen a man in the basement and went on to tell us that some of the other guests had experienced some seemingly paranormal events during the night as well. One guest had one bar of soap disappear and another re-wrapped itself. And another guest had a difficult time sleeping. As it happens, we caught up with that guest and her daughter—they both had a story to tell....

As it turns out, the guest who had trouble sleeping found it difficult because her bed began to shake and she would wake up unable to breathe, as if something were closing her airway. This was similar to our not being able to sleep and Katie's reports of breathing difficulty. Beyond this, the guest's daughter later reported a sighting not in the hotel itself but on the streets of Jerome. While doing some shopping the following morning, she saw a woman in a white lace dress walking down the street and disappearing into the side of a building. This spot turned out to be Husbands' Alley, named such as it used to lead into the red light district and apparently frequented by husbands tomcatting about. The alley is commemorated by a plaque on the wall with a photograph of a prostitute wearing a white lace dress. Further research into the Connor and its activity revealed that the hotel had burned down twice, and people often have difficulty sleeping...as well as having their objects and items moved about.

It is almost becoming a mantra at this point, but again we see almost ridiculously ordinary impressions or seemingly insignificant feelings turning into hits. It is the nature of sensory replication as your goal is to be able to experience reported activity to lend credence to the activity's authenticity. This includes even the smallest of feelings and impressions, and again, nothing should ever be ignored.

Listening to the stories and accounts of our fellow guests, it is clear that the Connor is very active. If three sets of guests each have experiences in the same night, then that would certainly suggest that the consistency and frequency of activity is fairly prolific. The nature of the activity is pretty diverse as well, so it becomes something of the luck of the draw whether you will see a lady wandering around or have your toiletries tampered with, but the chances are good that if you are looking for something out of the ordinary happening, you've come to the right place.

THE JEROME GRAND HOTEL
www.jeromegrandhotel.net
P.O. Box H, Jerome, AZ 86333
(928) 634-8200
(888) 817-6788

Hours of Operation: Hotel lobby is open and staffed twenty-four hours a day. Gift shop hours are 7 a.m. to 9 p.m. Located on the premises is the Asylum restaurant. The restaurant is open daily for lunch 11 a.m. to 3 p.m., and dinner from 5 to 9 p.m.

Directions: Same directions as the Connor Hotel. Hotel is located at the very top of Jerome. Hotel driveway is extremely narrow and looks like a sidewalk. The ride to the top of the hill is steep, and sufficient parking is available surrounding the hotel. Do not park too close to the edge. Use parking brake. Unsure of the availability of bus or cab service if car should plummet.

Intensity of paranormal activity: Moderate to high

Situated at the top of the mountain town that is Jerome, the Grand Hotel is without a doubt the most well-known haunted place in a town of haunted places. Anywhere you go in the town, when you mention that you are interested in the paranormal, you will be asked, "Did you go up to the Grand yet?" Built in 1926 as the United Verde Hospital, the building cuts an imposing image, as it is quite large and very ominous.

It sits high atop Cleopatra Hill, and occupies its space with a palpable sense of foreboding.

Though we did not stay at the Grand Hotel this time due to some scheduling issues, we did stop by and asked to look around. We were permitted to go up to the second floor and look around a bit, but that was the extent of it. If you are actually staying in the hotel you're obviously afforded much more freedom to roam and, I imagine, much more open conversation about the hauntings.

The Ghosts...

As you might expect, a building that started life as a hospital is bound to have its share of life and death within its walls. Guests staying at the Grand have reported sounds of tubercular coughing and moaning, footsteps up and down the hallways, cold spots, and the occasional sighting of one of its several ghostly residents.

Katie's Journal...

It is pretty widely known that anyone visiting Jerome should stay at the Jerome Grand if they want to experience something paranormal. Even though scheduling conflicts prevented an overnight investigation during our most recent trip to Jerome, our collection of previous experiences certainly makes for compelling evidence, and to not include information about this imposing landmark would be akin to writing a book about Parisian tourist attractions and not including the Eiffel Tower.

My experience with the hotel was in March of 2005. As a paranormal investigator, I could think of nothing more that I could possibly want to do for my birthday than to spend a night in the scariest hotel in Arizona. Perhaps that is an exaggeration, but it's probably not too far from the truth. This imposing monolith is likely the first thing to which a person's eyes are drawn when approaching Jerome, and it is visible for more miles than I can readily calculate. Its presence upon Cleopatra Hill commands the attention of anyone within sight, and gazing at it for any length of time feels more like a staring contest as you can almost feel it glowering back.

The drive to the hotel requires intense concentration, and I couldn't help but notice that the precarious driveway is almost as scary as the ghosts that drew me to the hotel in the first place. We found a parking space just a few feet from a sheer drop and made triple sure that the parking brake was engaged.

We checked in to the hotel and explained that we wanted to see a ghost. They were quite accommodating to our odd request and gave us a little bit of the history of the hotel. They even loaned us a copy of the video that featured the Jerome Grand on a popular syndicated show about the paranormal. The original Otis elevator delivered us to the third floor and we walked to our room at the end of the hallway. The room was perfectly lovely, with a king-size bed and a very large bathroom.

After puttering around Jerome, eating dinner, and waiting for night to fall, we returned to the hotel and set about our informal investigation. At the time, I was mainly interested in taking photos and seeing if anything anomalous appeared. We made a very thorough walk-through of all the common areas on each floor and returned to our room. Initially, I must have been entirely too excited to notice if I had any gut-level impressions of the hotel. The later it got, however, the more anxious I started to feel and I became aware of that very familiar feeling of not being alone. The more I tried to shrug it off, the more intense the feeling became, and I was actually beginning to dread going to bed. But the idea of being the only person left awake in the room was also extremely creepy, and I was not exactly thrilled at the prospect of a night of sleepless vigilance.

We tucked ourselves into bed and, per usual, Mikal took about three minutes to fall asleep, leaving me to enjoy the outdated copies of Newsweek left in the nightstand. I tried to keep distracted enough to actually fall asleep, but as the night wore on the room became as hot as an oven — especially odd given that it was about twenty-nine degrees outside and no one else seemed to notice (almost identical to my experience at the Connor Hotel). After several hours, I finally fell asleep.

At this point, I don't remember exactly what I dreamt while I was asleep, but I do recall that I thought it was odd. Even odder than the dreams was the experience I had as I was awakening. I was lying in the bed, more awake than asleep, and I heard a conversation between two women that — based on the volume of their voices — must have been standing right over me. Initially, I could not make out exactly what was being said, but I do distinctly recall hearing one woman say to the other, "Hurry up, Cynthia!" Hearing this made me open my eyes to find that there were no more people in my room than there were when I went to sleep, but I was no less certain of the conversation that had just taken place next to my bed. The hallway was still and quiet, and it was still entirely too early for any normal human being to be awake. I was indeed relieved when the sun finally started to shine, because as any self-respecting paranormal investigator would never admit, the sun makes the "scaries" go away.

The rest of our stay was uneventful, and we returned to our decidedly less haunted home. A review of our digital photos revealed numerous orbs, which I had expected. One photo, however, contained something rather unexpected. Since this trip was for my birthday, my kids had gone along. From the parking lot, I had taken a silly picture of my children who were looking down from the window of our room, sticking out their tongues, and acting goofy. When I loaded the picture onto my computer, I could see the photo in much greater detail, revealing not only my children, but also a very clearly defined female standing behind them. Could this have been the Cynthia that was observing us sleeping earlier in the day? *(Author's note: The photo can be seen at our website, www.wailingbansidhe.com)*

Given its history, and based on my experiences at the Jerome Grand, I would have to concur that it possesses an unusually high level of paranormal activity. This is a must-see for anyone with an interest in the paranormal (and an iron constitution), who wouldn't be scared off by the sounds of disembodied voices, or the desperate consumptive coughing of the long-deceased miners whose souls appear to be bound to forever roam its halls.

〰〰〰〰〰〰〰〰〰〰〰〰〰〰〰〰

Patrick's Journal...

The bulk of my experience with the Grand goes back to an investigation I attended several years ago with the Pima College Paranormal Investigation Group. We spent the night in the hotel and had access to pretty much all of it, including areas that were being renovated and, to my knowledge, are still inaccessible. While I am not at liberty to discuss the statistical findings of that investigation as they belong to the group's leader William Everist, I did have quite a few things that happened to me personally during the walk-through and overnight stay.

I've been doing this a long time and have investigated many locations and had a wide variety of experience throughout the years. One commonality to be found, however, is that while I will eventually get a creepy or uneasy feeling, I never get flat out scared. That changed with the Grand.

Before doing any official walk-through with the group, we were taken on a tour. This included the maintenance office, the unfinished fourth floor, and a wing of the hotel that included the old operating theater. We had a fairly large group and, when it came time to go up to the fourth floor, not all of us could fit in the elevator at one time. Half of our group piled in and half waited on the second floor.

I found myself in the back of the tightly packed elevator, flanked by Nicole and Ellen, my friends and frequent investigation partners. At about halfway up to the fourth floor I heard a scream coming from below the elevator down the shaft. I immediately thought it was someone in the other half of the group having a laugh and I looked around expecting to find others laughing as well. Ellen wore a similar smile to mine but both our smiles quickly turned to bewilderment when no one else in the elevator was acknowledging anything. I asked Nicole if she heard the scream and she said, "What?" No one in or waiting for the elevator heard the noise, confirmed the next morning as we compared notes. When we told the management, they informed us that a maintenance worker who lived in the apartment in the maintenance office had killed himself by letting the elevator crush his head. There was some disagreement at the time about the veracity of this claim, however, as a decent investigation was never launched and some of the details seemed suspect. Indeed, I stood at the bottom of the elevator shaft and watched it come down and he would most likely have died of old age before the elevator reached him. Add to that reports of two scalpel incisions behind his ears and you have the makings of a potential homicide.

Later on the tour, we encountered the operating theater and there was an old scrub room off to the side of it that I attempted to enter several times, but each time felt such a palpable sense of dread that I couldn't set more than a foot into it. Sure, this could be the product of an overactive imagination augmented by a heightened sense of spookiness, but it was simply impossible to convince myself to actually go in the room. I am not sure what relevance this has, if any, to the activity in the place, but I found it very odd, to say the least.

After the official walk-through portion, we retreated to our rooms for the night, dream journals at the bedside in hopes of having images of ghosts dancing in our heads. Nicole and I shared a room and both of us had a big problem with the bathroom. In the walk-through, I had felt the same way and I learned the next morning that most people on the investigation shared my feelings. It was bad enough that we couldn't bear to have the door open. It's important to mention that normally when I say things like, "I felt uneasy with…" or "I had a problem with…", I am not talking about a malevolent force or anything that feels negative. Very rarely when I investigate do I come across a location that I feel is bad or evil. The feelings I got from the bathroom, however, were not at all friendly.

During the night, the collective team reported hearing someone walking along the outside balcony all at the same time. The consistency suggested that someone was, in fact, walking out there. The catch to that particular scenario is that the sounds were coming from the closed wing where no one should be. The hotel staff denied being over there, so it seemed a significant result.

Again, this all took place on an official investigation for Pima College, so many of the results cannot be shared here. Still, there were many reports of activity and many verifications of that activity. It is one of the few places that I would say you are almost guaranteed to yield results. That is a bold statement to make, but the place is very active and has certainly earned its reputation as the most haunted place in Jerome. Despite its inherent creepiness and a not-so-friendly feeling from the activity (and the fact that driving up there gives you a very real sense that a mistake could put you through the roof into someone's living room), this is one of my absolute favorite haunted places. It scared me when I was there...but has always made me want to go back.

The Liberty Theatre
www.jeromelibertytheater.com
110 Jerome Avenue, Jerome, AZ 86331
(928) 649-9016

Hours of Operation: Please call theatre for hours.
Directions: Same directions as Connor Hotel. Theatre is literally right next to the hotel.
Intensity of paranormal activity: Low

Immediately adjacent to the Connor Building is the Liberty Theatre. Mikal and I had visited this theatre previously, and based on an experience that Mikal had, we thought it would be a worthy addition to our ghostly chronicle, although this trip was really just a friendly visit rather than a full-scale investigation. The downstairs section of the theatre houses a gift shop with some of the coolest souvenirs available in all of Jerome. Upstairs is the newly remodeled theatre, which has been lovingly and painstakingly restored to its original glory.

On our previous visit, Mikal and I were enjoying the self-guided tour of the upstairs theatre. It may have been due to the inclement weather but, whatever the reason, there were notably fewer people visiting so we had the theatre to ourselves.

Because Mikal is such a Hollywood buff, we took pictures of the memorabilia and I happened to notice an orb in the photo. This did not surprise me because I am of the opinion that the entire town of Jerome is haunted, but I had no information regarding this theatre and I knew of no claims of paranormal activity. Nevertheless, I had my suspicions. We finished our tour of the theatre and began down the stairs to the gift shop. Mikal paused at the top of the stairs to take a few more pictures while I continued down the steps. I began to get impatient since he was taking quite a while, but when he finally came down the steps he said excitedly, "I just saw someone walk past me."

Knowing we were the only ones in the theatre at the time, we both walked back up the stairs to see if we had missed anyone. There was no one upstairs with us. The figure that Mikal had seen was dark and shadowy and completely non-corporeal. At the time we were just visiting as tourists and did not bother to make any inquiries regarding paranormal activity. This time, we decided to try and fill in those blanks.

We took the self-guided tour again, hoping to have a similar experience. This time, there were more people visiting so it would have been more difficult to duplicate that experience, but since we already had a firsthand account, we were more focused on gathering the information to substantiate what Mikal had seen. After completing the uneventful tour, we spoke to the proprietor and explained the purpose of our visit. Mikal relayed his experience to her, which pleasantly surprised her: "There is supposed to be a ghost upstairs, but I have never heard of anyone else that's seen it!"

Sadly, very little is known about the ghost of Liberty Theatre. There are no specific reports of any deaths associated with the theatre, but given Jerome's rough and colorful past, and the theatre's proximity to Husbands' Alley, it certainly is not surprising that even this unassuming tribute to early Hollywood should claim a spirit of its own.

TEMPE

CASEY MOORE'S OYSTER HOUSE

850 South Ash Avenue,
Tempe, AZ 85281
(480) 968-9935

Hours of Operation: Call for hours. Reservations recommended for Friday and Saturday night.

Directions: From I-10, take exit 153B for Broadway Road/52nd Street. Turn right at Broadway to Priest Drive. Turn left at Priest Drive and continue to University Drive. Turn right at University Drive and continue to Ash Avenue. Turn right on Ash Avenue. The restaurant will be easy to spot. Ample parking is available behind the restaurant, and the menu offers many tasty and modestly priced choices.

Intensity of paranormal activity: Moderate

Located in historic Tempe, Casey Moore's Oyster House boasts a menu of sumptuous seafood, free flowing refreshments, friendly employees, and horseradish sauce so hot you need to wash it down with wasabi to douse the flames.

Built in 1910, this popular watering hole began its life as the home of Mr. and Mrs. William Mouer. They lived the duration of their lives in this home, and eventually both died there. Since then, this building has had many different incarnations which include alleged use as a brothel during the 1930s and, later on, as a boarding house.

Among the residents of the boarding house, located at Ninth and Ash, was a young lady named Sarah. Not much is known about Sarah except that she lived briefly and died suddenly in her upstairs apartment. The circumstances surrounding her murder by strangulation are cloudy, and the common lore tells that she fell victim to a crime of passion by a man whose love she did not return.

The Ghosts...

Witnesses have reported numerous accounts of apparitions and poltergeist activity in the upstairs rooms, including the sounds of children playing, as well as the vision of a man and woman dressed in vintage clothing, tripping the light fantastic much to the shock and delight of several different occupants of the house across the street.

But it is the apparition of Sarah that has been commanding the most attention from employees and customers since her untimely death in 1966....

According to longtime manager Gavin Rutledge, Sarah has made her presence known to him since he began working there in the mid 1980s. "Before 1993 was sheer terror for me," Gavin recalls as he describes the frequency of his encounters with Sarah. Her propensity for throwing spoons and forks (thankfully, no knives), and office staplers has caused Gavin to run from the upstairs office on more than one occasion, often leaving behind the unfinished bookkeeping:

> *"I can't tell you what happens after something flies across the room...because I'm never in the room after that."*

In the years since 1993, Gavin's experiences with Sarah have been fewer and farther between, although they have not completely ceased. On the advice of a number of sensitives and paranormal experts, he began speaking to her in an attempt to help her move on, and that appears to have brought about a truce...at least for now.

Aside from the tasty menu and amiable pub-like atmosphere, Casey Moore's Oyster House has a great deal to offer the budding paranormal investigator. This is absolutely one restaurant that is not to be missed, be it for the food or the ghosts. After all, the regulars always return to enjoy the food and spirits, and the spirits return to enjoy the regulars.

Katie's Journal...

From an investigation standpoint, I would have to say that Casey Moore's is among the most active places I have ever been. From the very moment we entered the upstairs dining area, the sensation of not being alone was very strong. Let me reiterate that, as with all of our investigations, we had very little previous knowledge of the goings on inside of the building, or of the events that brought about the alleged paranormal activity. We went in with as clear a canvas as possible, and it did not take long to start painting a very frightening picture.

The upstairs area is very small. It consists of two dining rooms, a small storage closet with a gold damask curtain, a serving station, and a private office. As you reach the top of the stairs, one dining room is directly in front of you and one is to your immediate right. We gravitated towards the dining room to the right because it was slightly larger and quite a bit brighter. The décor of the room included light floral wallpaper, which gave it a rather cheerful feeling. We made ourselves at home, and set about the walk-through portion of the investigation. As I stepped out of the flower-patterned room, I made my way to the entrance of the other dining room. As I passed through the doorway, the mood immediately changed from cheerful to a much heavier and somewhat sinister feeling. I felt as though someone was standing directly in front of me as I entered the room and, as if on cue, the EMF detector began sounding its alarm and gave a reading that buried the needle. A thorough search for anything else that could possibly give such a high reading yielded nothing out of the ordinary, so...the game was afoot.

The room is square shaped, and is large enough to hold four tables. In the back of the room there is a small area that is set back from the rest of the room, preventing the room from being a perfect square. It was to that corner that I instantly and inexplicably felt drawn. I stepped into the cubby and my gut reaction was one of complete shock and surprise, like the time when I was a small child and pulled my bedroom curtain back to peek outside—only to find our insane neighbor peering in my window. At the same time, I felt compelled to stare into the hallway at the small closet. It felt as though those two things were somehow connected, although I could find no specific reason for the connection. For lack of a better description, it felt distinctly as though I were being cornered.

For the first part of the investigation, we refrained from conversation and recorded our individual impressions for later comparison. I made spotty, one-line observations while Patrick chose to make notes on a floorplan that he had drawn in his notebook. Since the area was so small, we found that it did not take long to cover the entire area and note our initial impressions. Upon comparison, Patrick and I discovered that we had made remarkably similar notes, down to the specific feelings of abject horror in the small cubby area and its connection to the small closet. Even Mikal had to admit that he wouldn't want to be alone in that room for any extended length of time.

With initial feelings recorded, we shifted our focus to the photographs that Mikal was taking and wondered if we could intensify the results by turning off the lights. Patrick and I stayed in the dining room comparing notes while Mikal went to get the bartender to show us where the controls were located. He returned with Kyle, who asked us, "Do you know the story?" Mikal told him that we hadn't yet had the chance to talk to Gavin, when Kyle then pointed to the cubby in the corner and said, "She was murdered right over there." (The "she" we would later learn was Sarah.) Reacting like truly consummate professionals, it was very difficult to hide our unmitigated excitement over such a direct and accurate hit. We later spoke with Gavin and compared our experiences to his. Certainly, after two decades of playing hide and seek with Sarah, Gavin has had his share of frights, including one instance of an upstairs dining table being thrown on its side.

From my observation, Casey Moore's is most assuredly a hotbed of paranormal experience. From the information we gathered, Casey Moore's seems to be exhibiting activity relating to both an apparition (who definitely wants to get noticed) and a true ballroom dancing-style haunting. If you want great food and great ghost stories, Casey Moore's is definitely worth a visit.

Patrick's Journal...

Upon entering the upstairs dining area, you are met with a couple of directional options. To the right there is a long room with tables on either side, and almost straight ahead you'll find a smaller, more boxlike room with a cubby set into the far left end. The two rooms are separated by a small hallway, which contains a closet with a dumbwaiter, a wait station, and an office at the far left end.

We set up initially in the long room to the right. Following the abbreviated sensory replication model of our particular operation, we moved throughout the rooms taking note of any odd feelings or sensations. Given that there were only two rooms (to explore in this case), the initial walk-through took very little time. Still, the room across from the stairs kept drawing us back in time and time again.

When entering that room, I was met with an almost palpable sense of dread, dizziness, and just the general feeling of not being alone. The room seemed absolutely clogged with activity and it felt as if it were swirling around. Even with all that emotional noise in the room, I found myself drawn into the cubby in the corner. It seemed an odd addition to the room, but if pressed, I couldn't give a terribly good reason as to why it was commanding so much attention.

Approaching the corner, the air in the room became stuffy and it was hard to breathe. I found myself feeling a combination of fear and anger. Certainly odd, but the tricky part of this process is to filter out expectation and imagination and focus on what is really there. Not knowing anything about the activity in a place is one of the best ways to combat this, but obviously your imagination can still run wild. Even given this and the almost ridiculous level of sensations I was getting, I marked on my crudely scrawled map all of the locations where I felt things and specifically what I felt.

We spent about two and a half hours in the rooms, with the majority of time spent in the smaller room. Any time we left and moved to the other room we found ourselves drawn back to the room with the cubby. One such time found me in the room to get the sound recorder we'd left, and just on a whim, I leaned in the cubby with the EMF detector to get some extra readings. In doing so, I caught movement out of the corner of my eye in the hallway. It was a silhouette of a person moving from the closet across the hall toward the office. Moving quickly into the hallway, I found Katie and Mikal in the other room and no one else was in the hallway.

Based on my apparent apparition sighting, we decided to see what it would look like if the lights were off. While Mikal went downstairs to obtain permission to extinguish the lights, Katie and I went to the cubby and stood there as I explained what I'd been doing when I saw the figure. We talked about the cubby and how odd it was that it was constantly drawing attention. This was about the time when Mikal returned with Kyle, the bartender, who asked us if we were being drawn to that corner. Katie answered that we were in fact drawn to it and asked if there was something going on there. Kyle smiled and said, "Yeah, that's where she was murdered."

Mikal – apparently interviewing a lamp in the notorious cubby – while a curious orb looks on.

As you know from the above history section, the primary offender of the activity was a college-aged girl who was strangled to death by a jealous lover in her bed, which happened to be in the cubby. Over the years a great deal of activity has been centered on the room, and one constant seems to be feelings of not being alone and general feelings of uneasiness. Upon further interviewing, we found that many people have seen a figure walking from the closet to the office as well. At one time, the closet was a water closet-style bathroom and it was fairly common for men washing up in the sink to see the image of the murdered girl in the mirror.

As far as personal experience goes, this particular investigation provided one of the most profound results I have ever experienced. From seeing an apparition and verifying the activity to replicating several feelings and experiences throughout the room, this place was hot on the night we were there. The upstairs dining room is generally open Friday and Saturday nights, and the room across the hall is definitely where the action takes place. Given the quality of food and the level of activity, you could do much, much worse than Casey Moore's, and there aren't a whole lot of places you could do better.

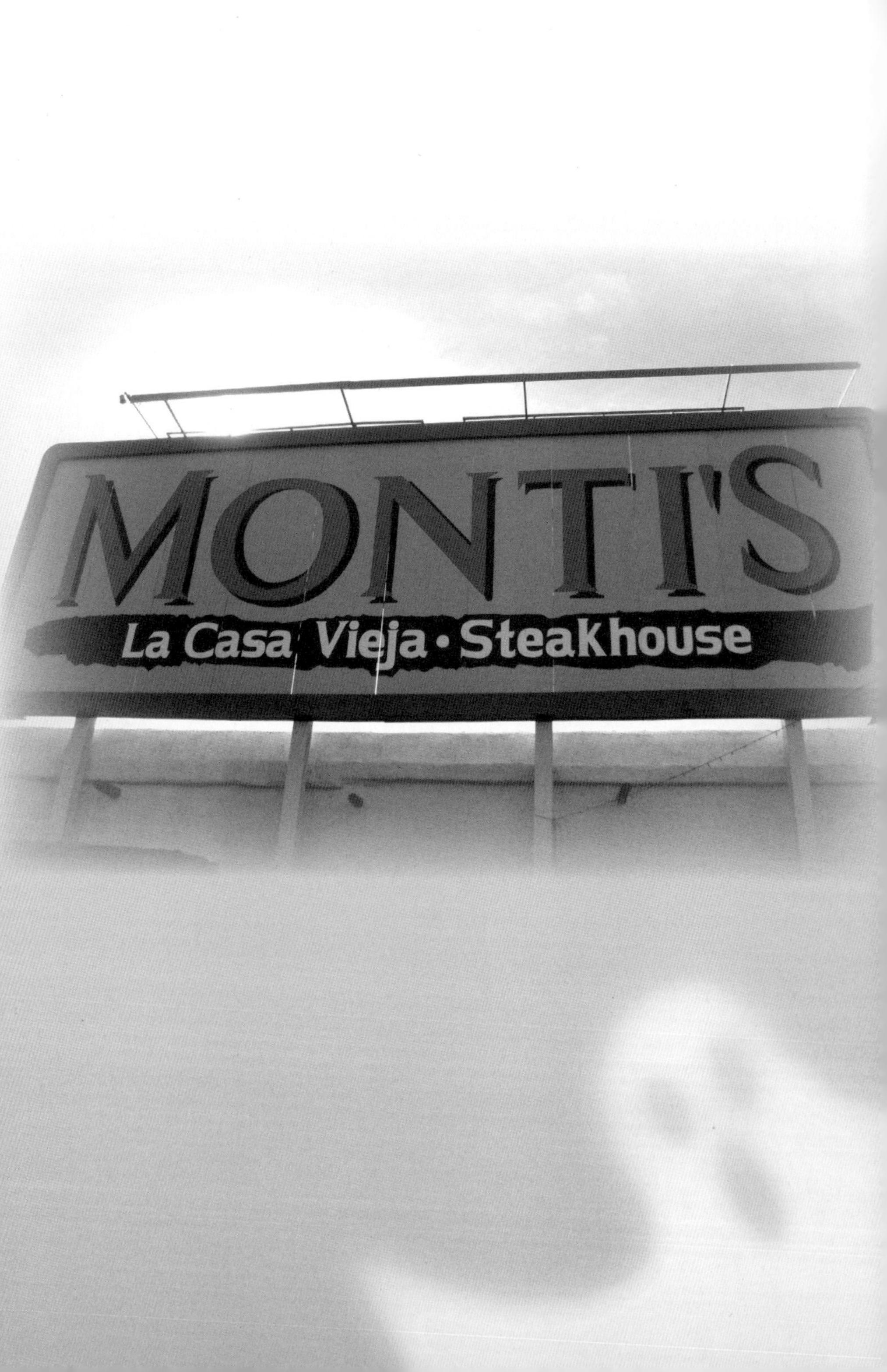
MONTI'S
La Casa Vieja · Steakhouse

MONTI'S LA CASA VIEJA RESTAURANT

www.montis.com

100 South Mill Avenue,

Tempe, AZ 85281

(480) 967-7594

Hours of Operation: Sunday through Thursday, 11 a.m. to 10 p.m.; Friday and Saturday, 11 a.m. to 11 p.m.

Directions: From I-10, take exit 153B for Broadway Road/52nd Street. Turn right at Broadway to Priest Drive. Turn left at Priest to University Drive. Turn right at University Drive to Mill Avenue. Turn left at Mill Avenue. The restaurant will be easy to spot. Ample parking is available adjacent to the restaurant, and the menu offers outstanding steakhouse fare at moderate prices.

Intensity of paranormal activity: Moderate

Built in Tempe long before there was a Tempe, Monti's La Casa Vieja is the longest continuously occupied building in Phoenix and its various suburbs and satellites. The restaurant occupies a sprawling 11,000 square feet, and is absolutely packed with history. Boasting the original adobe walls and the oldest ocotillo roof of its kind in the city, this is one of the most authentic historical buildings you are likely to find. The original hacienda style house was built in 1871 by Charles Turnbull Hayden to allow for the opening of a flour mill and ferry service used for crossing the Salt River. When Hayden married in 1876, he and his wife converted the home into something of an all-purpose outpost offering a hotel, post office, general store and blacksmithing shop. The outpost became known as Hayden's Ferry, which became its own community centered mostly on the mill and hacienda.

In a historical side note: A year after the conversion of the home to community housing and marketplace, the Haydens were blessed with a son, Carl, who was born in the hacienda and eventually became Sheriff, cavalry soldier, and congressman. He ultimately served in the House and Senate for more than fifty-seven years.

It wasn't until late in the 1880s that the community was renamed Tempe based upon the suggestion of an English nobleman who thought it resembled the Vale of Tempe in Greece.

In the 1890s the house earned the title La Casa Vieja, or "the old house," when the family moved from the hacienda to a new house. After the move, the restaurant was added onto the house, again servicing the mill, and continued to be run by the Hayden daughters until it was sold in the 1930s. The property changed hands many times over the next twenty or so years until it was taken over by Leonard F Monti, Sr., in 1954. He opened the restaurant in 1956, adding his name to the title but keeping La Casa Vieja to keep with history and tradition.

Monti's has been in the family since then and it has been lovingly cared for and restored, providing support to the structure and even adding the old mill warehouses to its floor plan. The open-air section in the center of the hacienda has been covered and converted to a dining room with the original water fountain still intact and operational. Historical artifacts and documents line the walls and there are many sections of that wall covered by clear glass to show the original adobe inside. The menu is outstanding, and they easily have some of the best clam chowder in the history of seafood.

The Ghosts...

Over the years there has been quite a bit of paranormal activity. It's an old place with an abundance of history, and it seems a fair amount of that history isn't content to be displayed on the walls. From spectral cowboys to adding machines that do work on their own, the place has a lot to offer the would-be ghost-hunter. Phantom voices have been heard, sounds of children playing and laughing around the fountain are common, and certain bathroom stalls have been known to shake. This is a place of not-so-living history and it wants to be told whatever way it can. With an incredible atmosphere, equally incredible steaks, and an abundance of activity, Monti's proves that Tempe may very well be Phoenix's hottest spot for hauntings.

Katie's Journal...

My first impression of Monti's was, "Wow, this place is HUGE." When we arrived, we were greeted very warmly and enthusiastically by Michael Monti himself and given a brief tour of the facilities, mostly to get our bearings. Since this establishment is as much a museum as it is a restaurant, it would be impossible to take in all the artwork and artifacts documented throughout every room of its formidable 11,000 square feet. We were given maps to help us along the way, and Mr. Monti pointed us in the direction of the oldest part of the building, the Hayden Room.

My initial feeling of the Hayden Room was very comfortable and welcoming. It was as though the Hayden family had invited me to sit for awhile, and I gladly accepted. I made my way past the Indian Room towards the area where the old building meets the new building. I paused for a moment to marvel at the original construction, which predates me by a full century, and I suddenly had the overwhelming, if not dizzying, sensation that I was not alone. Technically, I was not alone as Mikal was rummaging through a bag to find his copy of the map, but I felt as though all eyes were on me...and my every move was being monitored with great anticipation. This was my first real indication of the level of activity present in the restaurant.

Not being familiar with the floor plan and struggling to orientate myself, I continued heading south towards the hallway known as Diablo Way, a long passage whose walls are lined with friendly caricatures of statesmen and others of great historical significance. Juggling the map, the notebook, and the EMF detector, I entered the Hacienda Room. I was still acutely aware of the sensation that I had an unseen escort, so I was not in any big hurry to drop all of my equipment and send it skittering into the darkness of the vast dining hall, turning a well-planned investigation into a slapstick routine and betraying my cool exterior. Fortunately, I did not have to concern myself for very long because the moment I stepped into the room the EMF detector went off, lighting the room like an underground rave and giving an unusually high reading. In fact, like Casey Moore's, the reading was off the chart. What I found most peculiar about this reading was that it was solid throughout the entire room. This reading alone does not bring any certainty to the claims of paranormal activity; however, I could find no reason — inside or out — for the high level of electromagnetic energy.

By this time, I could hear Patrick and Mikal close by, and I finally had my bearings. I mentioned the EMF reading to Patrick and he recalled a similar incident from a previous investigation of Monti's led by parapsychologist Bill Everist. Patrick had encountered Bill in that room, puzzling over the unusually high EMF readings he was getting, and neither he nor the rest of the group could determine a natural cause.

Moving forward, we continued the walk-through of the restaurant together, as it became much easier to navigate the maze en masse. Patrick took over the job of monitoring EMF readings and Mikal continued to take photos. As we moved through the next few rooms, Patrick and I both noticed that the EMF detector would occasionally flash. Not the normal constant reading that is usually recorded, but just one or two quick and random flashes. It was just enough for both of us to wonder aloud, "Did that just flash, or was it my imagination?" We began pausing briefly after every few steps and realized it was flashing, but only flickering a little. It was as though something was darting around or rushing past. This was most prominent in the Fountain Room, an area that once served as an outdoor gathering place for the tenants of the building, aptly named for the original garden fountain that is now the centerpiece of the room.

An orb in the Fountain Room at Monti's.

Our "tour" took us on through the Zane Grey Room, a lodge-style banquet hall; the adjacent Frontier Room, and into the Juice Room. Once a storage area for beverages, the Juice Room has been converted into a dining area. Its walls are simple and white, with one small part of the original wall visible through glass. The few antiques in this room include an old clock and an antique rifle, but even in its deliberate simplicity, there is an overwhelmingly frightening feeling about this room. Even as an investigator, there are places that I would not want to be left alone for any great length of time. This is definitely one of them. There were no abnormal readings, no fantastic swirls of light, no demonic voices instructing us to get out...just a terribly frightening feeling. Even Michael Monti admitted that he has been afraid in that room since childhood.

We moved through the Juice Room and into the adjacent waiting area. As I stood in the waiting area, I gazed through the doorway to the room at the back of the building, the Senator's Room. The Senator's Room is appointed in a simple, stately fashion, with an original fireplace at the far end and pale-colored walls providing a backdrop for photos depicting a bygone era. As I approached the Senator's Room, my sense of being followed intensified. There was a palpable buzz of energy that grew stronger with each step I took, and when I entered the room, the energy abruptly stopped. It was the same awkward feeling as when someone enters the wrong room, disrupting a meeting filled with high powered executives, only to have the activity come screeching to a halt as all eyes turn towards the embarrassed intruder. The only difference being the obvious fact that, for all intents and purposes, this room was empty.

As the walk-through portion of our investigation was nearing completion, we retraced our steps through the Juice Room, exiting on the other side in the Frontier Room. We managed to pick up another EMF reading that started outside the Juice Room and stopped at a nearby booth. As we surveyed the immediate area for possible causes, I turned my gaze towards the Zane Grey Room. For the briefest moment, I could have sworn I saw a man standing in the doorway wearing a cowboy hat and a vest, just watching us. My first instinct was to dismiss it completely as a figment of my imagination, but then I remembered why I was there to begin with, and jotted it down in my notes.

During the post-walk-through discussion, Patrick and I found that we had a few major hits with our impressions. Between us, we both felt as though we were being followed, and we both had the same intense feelings that we had caused an unwelcome disruption in the Senator's Room. Impressive, but certainly not enough to draw any conclusions.

We discussed this with Michael Monti, and he began to describe the experiences that had been reported to him by employees and customers. People have seen and heard children in the Fountain Room, he explained. Patrick and I quickly exchanged a puzzled look, and explained to Mr. Monti the EMF readings we had gotten in that room. At the time, we thought it strange that something would be passing by so quickly, but it made more sense after learning that children had been seen running about.

Satisfied that we had gotten a decent amount of evidence to support the notion that Monti's has had its share of paranormal activity, we began to wrap up the interview portion of the investigation. As we gathered our things, Mr. Monti recalled another experience reported by an employee several years ago. The restaurant was undergoing renovations (a perfect time for the ghosts to come out) and the front portion of the building was completely off-limits for safety reasons. Disregarding the posted signs, one cavalier young man wandered back there to impress his young lady friend. His adventure was brought to an abrupt halt as he turned to look back, and seated in a bench in the adjacent waiting area was a man dressed in cowboy attire who looked at him as if to say, "You best be goin' now, son," and he did just that — quickly.

Was this the same cowboy that I saw in the Zane Grey Room? I excitedly recalled the man that I had seen earlier in the evening, but had dismissed as an active imagination. Now, it seems, this could be the biggest hit of the entire investigation. Is this a phantom cowboy, vigilantly keeping watch over his old homestead? If so, he certainly does a good job of keeping the peace.

Patrick's Journal...

Upon entering Monti's, it's impossible not to be struck with a sense of history. The lobby and waiting areas are filled with articles and artifacts from years gone by, ready to acclimate you to this dauntingly old establishment. There is a buzz about the place that is immediately apparent, and I found myself enthralled by the atmosphere right away. Because of its size, you need a two-sided floor plan to navigate the whole of the place. It's 11,000 square feet of rooms and corridors, all packed with treasures from the past.

I started my "tour" going through the Mural Room and down the length of that side of the restaurant. It led me to a long dining room with a picture of Carl Hayden on the wall at the far end, called the Senator's Room. Entering that room feels not unlike entering a room full of people who turn and look at you, making you feel awkward for having interrupted whatever was going on. Every time I went in there I felt that sense of interruption and of being watched.

Coming back out, I retraced my steps and went in the Juice Room, another long private dining room with paintings and an old rifle mounted on the wall. Immediately I felt somewhat stuffy in the room and I wanted very much to get out. It just seems to carry an uneasy feeling with it and is not the most pleasant of rooms in Monti's.

From there I exited through a door leading into the Frontier Room and moved on to the Fountain Room. The Fountain Room is a large area that was once an open-air courtyard and still holds the fountain built in 1920. This room again felt somewhat busy, and there was a definite sense of someone else being there. This feeling permeated the surrounding rooms including the Zane Grey Room. Moving back across the Fountain Room and through the bar, I crossed over into the newer additions to the restaurant.

One word about the bar, I didn't get anything significant from it myself. Indeed the cleaning crew and the country music being pumped in from the ceiling-mounted speakers didn't make it easy to get impressions in that room, but it has been the site of some reported activity after closing. It has a buzz about it, but I can't say for certain if that is anything out of the ordinary or just the feeling one gets from a well-lit room with music and boisterous activity. Still it should be noted that this area potentially holds more than one kind of spirit.

Getting over to the newer portions, it all seemed fairly quiet and peaceful. There is still a strong sense of historical ambiance, but the feelings of not being alone were absent. Going down Diablo Way, however, brings you to the Hacienda Room. I entered that room and again felt a strong sense of something. This room is strange because it tends to give butterflies and a non-distinct feeling of something odd. I found myself coming back to this room a few times, exiting and going down the hallway, and then coming back in. Sitting in the dark in the back of the room, it's hard not to feel that odd creepiness and again, while not distinct enough to put a finger on, the feeling is palpable. Indeed, if creepy feelings had a thickness to them, you'd be able to climb up it like a mountain.

An orb waits to be seated in the Hacienda Room at Monti's. Could this be the cause of the unusually high EMF readings?

After a time of flittering in and out of this room, I reconnected with Katie and Mikal. I asked Katie to bring the EMF detector in to see if we could get any unusual readings. The EMF detector stayed a solid red the entire time. We searched the room and surrounding area for some source of the readings, but nothing seemed to be causing it. Indeed later when interviewing owner Michael Monti about the activity, we confirmed that there was nothing that should be causing the readings.

Monti's office does share a wall with the room, but the EMF didn't flash at all up against that wall nor out in the hallway closer to the office. The readings we were getting in the middle of the room didn't correspond with anything electronic at all. This echoed a previous investigation of Monti's that I was a part of, and while the feelings one experiences in a room can be misinterpreted or colored by familiarity, EMF readings cannot be influenced in that way.

The three of us made another full circuit of the restaurant and again I felt the same sort of things I had felt previously. When we compared notes, Katie and I found that we had marked many of the same feelings and impressions of the same rooms. Again connecting with Monti at the end of the walk-through, we found that we were scoring a fair amount of hits.

I personally didn't have any really huge things happen here, it was mostly just the impressions and feelings I got from the rooms but those seemed to significantly correspond with my fellow investigators and with reported activity. Many times, this is what paranormal investigations are: getting a few experiences that match previously reported ones. It doesn't have to be seeing things fly across the room or seeing an apparition dancing the cha-cha. A positive result is a positive result, and Monti's offered up many of them.

This is simply one of the coolest places you could choose to dine. The atmosphere is great and the information and history around is a blessing to anyone interested. Diners are invited to speak with the staff about the history and artifacts, and many of the house's former tenants still come in for meals and to look around. Monti's La Casa Vieja is a dream for the casual investigator because the staff invites you to look around and ask questions and even gives you a floor plan to help you on the way. Monti's is a must-visit for anyone looking for good food, good atmosphere, and good activity.

TUCSON

22ND STREET ANTIQUE MALL
www.22ndstreetantiquemall.com
5302 East 22nd Street Tucson, AZ 85711
(520) 514-5262

Hours of Operation: Monday through Friday, 10 a.m. to 5 p.m. and Sunday, 11 a.m. to 4 p.m.

Directions: From I-10, take exit 259 at 22nd Street/Starr Pass Boulevard. Merge onto South Freeway and turn left at 22nd Street. 22nd Street Antique Mall is located just west of 22nd and Craycroft streets. Sufficient parking is available in front of the antique mall. Be sure and bring lots of money with you because in addition to the ghosts, you will undoubtedly find a collectible that you can't live without!

Intensity of paranormal activity: Moderate

Beginning life in the 1960s as Mitchell's Furniture, 22nd Street Antiques in Tucson is a sprawling store claiming some 15,000 square feet of real estate. Currently owned by Paul and Myra Rees, as it has been for the past fifteen years, the store is divided into multiple rooms, including an annexed area with closed-off upstairs space. The floor is divided into rows of paddock-like booths where the various dealers set up their wares. The items on display are varied and plentiful, representing many different time periods and cultures, and making the space a sort of melting pot of history from around the world. It's not difficult to see how such a place would be rife with activity.

And rife with activity it is....

According to long-time employees Judy and Kathy, there have been many disturbances over the past several years. Not only has there been a lot of activity, the mode and function of the activity reported varies as much as the items on sale from booth to booth.

The Ghosts...

The upstairs area has been closed off for two years, so there is little activity there now, but when it was used in the past as a functioning part of the store, that was certainly not the case. In booth 52, a photograph of a woman was seen and heard tapping itself on the window until its eventual purchase. In another booth, which housed office equipment, a typewriter would tap away on its own. A radio in the area would turn itself up, forcing workers to have to come upstairs to turn it off, only to find the volume going back up as soon as they went back downstairs. Customers were also known to flee the upstairs with claims that it was haunted.

Perhaps the most profound of the activity upstairs, however, are the claims of sightings of two separate ghosts. Judy reports that one had a habit of doing somersaults down the rows of booths...only to disappear right in front of her. The other, reported by both Judy and Kathy, had a tendency to hide behind pillars, as if playing some spectral game of hide-and-seek.

The annexed area downstairs also has its pair of ghostly figures. At one time a booth in the back right corner housed a collection of Victorian-era items, and on several occasions, Judy saw a woman in a period dress complete with bustle that stood in the booth and waved just a little through crossed arms. Kathy reports a run-in with a playful spirit who liked to run past and brush her arm mischievously.

Beyond this cheerful archway in 22nd Street Antiques, customers
and staff have found that the antiques have a life of their own.

The main building, while not complemented with ghostly figures as much, has certainly had its own share of goings on. The activity here seems to be centered on booths that contained items from recently deceased dealers. During the time between the deaths of the dealers and the removal of their items, the store's workers report a variety of activity from laughter to items moving of their own accord. In one instance, workers in the back office heard a loud crash from up front as if a booth had spilled its contents to the floor. When they rushed out to investigate, they found the booth to be untouched and unspoiled.

Activity continues in the back room area, which is off-limits and is where the breaker boxes are located. Unlike the rest of the store's happenings, the spirit occupying this back area carries with it a certain sense of dread. Judy and Kathy both feel like it's the only one that is really scary and whose intentions are anything other than playful. The back room's occupant has been seen by the store staff on several occasions and seems to be less than friendly.

The store plays host to the full gamut of paranormal activity from apparitions to haunting phenomena to poltergeist activity. In some ways, reported activity seems to run counter to the more accepted definitions of each category, but, as was stated earlier, there are no hard and fast rules to any of this and any classification is just a working theory. The clarity of the accounts and the support of more than one witness lends credence to the claims, and a person's attachment to their belongings, even things they sell, makes it more likely that a person would be tied to them after death. The staff at the store is enormously friendly, and while there are some areas that are off limits to the public, there are plenty of accessible areas with reported activity to check out. The addition of myriad items on sale makes this a great bet for an afternoon of shopping and amateur ghost-hunting. You'll definitely leave with a great experience.

〜〜〜〜〜〜〜〜〜〜

Katie's Journal...

Not all haunted buildings are gothic-style mansions set high atop foreboding hilltops, surrounded by imposing wrought iron. Some buildings that report an abundance of paranormal activity are hidden in plain sight. Such is the case of 22nd Street Antiques.

We arrived at closing and were greeted rather excitedly by the very friendly staff. We explained the process and began the walk-through portion of the investigation. The store is comprised of two separate buildings connected by an archway. For no particular reason, I decided to head towards the two-story annex on the east side of the building. As I passed through the archway, I felt an instant heaviness in my chest and a dizzy, lightheaded sensation. "Bingo!" I thought to myself, and immediately made notes. In the center of the room is a wide staircase, and with each step I took closer to the stairs, the more intense the feelings became. Naturally, I followed the sensation up the stairs to the second floor.

A now vacant area, the second floor was once filled with merchandise and, as I later found out, was frequently the scene of many unexplained occurrences. Although the initial heavy feeling felt like a bag of cement being thrust at my midsection, by the time I reached the top of the stairs, it had leveled off but had by no means disappeared. I circled the top floor, stopping at each empty booth, carefully recording each impression and feeling. As I walked towards the back of the building, I stopped at the only booth in the back that has a window. I found myself suddenly feeling anxious and impatient, so I made a note of that and marked the booth number, 52, in my notes. I completed my walk-through of the upstairs, but I was not able to shake the feeling that I was moving through molasses or that my head might, at any second, spin off of my neck like some deranged children's toy.

Making my way downstairs, I circled the same path through the lower portion. As with the upstairs, the feelings of heaviness intensified as I approached the back of the building and I made notes of such. It was almost like an electrical charge buzzing through the air. The three booths at the back of the downstairs area had a decidedly occupied sense, and I am not referring to the merchandise. I completed the walk-through on the first floor of the annex and passed again through the archway, returning to the main selling floor. In that instant, the feeling of heaviness vanished and I no longer felt that my brain was spinning wildly out of control.

The rest of this building had the same combination of energies that one might expect in any antique store, likely the result of residual energy. Not even something that would be classified as paranormal, necessarily, just the normal nostalgic feeling of history mixing with pop culture. As I neared the back of the building, I once again began feeling the intense heaviness that I had experienced in the annex, although not quite as strong. In the very back of the store is a set of double doors that allows entry to the warehouse. This warehouse is not open to the public, but we were permitted to enter for the purpose of investigating. As with the annex, I passed through the double doors and it felt like a vise grip to the solar plexus. I could not help but immediately notice the collection of breaker boxes on the rear wall. This is relevant because electromagnetic energy has long been believed to be an indicator of paranormal activity and the presence of such equipment can either exacerbate or interfere with the EMF readings and corrupt the data on an investigation. Science aside, the warehouse was scary—partially because of the life-size Halloween mannequins and partially because of the overwhelming feeling of an unseen entity. Noting all of these impressions, I completed my walk-through and returned to the front of the store.

Among those present for the investigation were two of the store employees, Judy and Kathy. Now that we had notes to compare, Judy led us on a tour of the "hot spots" and it came as no surprise to me that she would make a beeline for the annex. She led us through the archway and up the stairs, explaining that when the booths were occupied, employees would frequently hear the sound of typewriter keys emanating from a grouping of vintage office furniture. She went on to describe another grouping of furniture at the back of the store, procured from the estate of an elderly woman. Included was a dining table with chairs that seemed to constantly be moved by unseen hands, and a picture of the furniture's owner that would rattle insistently against the window glass as if to demand, "Pay attention to me!" Knowing that there was only one booth at the back with a window, I showed everyone my notes from the walk-through indicating my impressions of booth 52 and they confirmed that it was the very same booth.

On the heels of that direct hit, we followed the group downstairs. We made a few stops at booths with reports of activity, but the events in question appeared to be related to the individual dealers who had passed away over the years. In the interim between their deaths and the removal of their items, several people reported unusual experiences. I had no such impressions in any of these booths, but more than one person reported similar experiences during the short duration of this specific activity.

Moving to the back of the building, we approached the ominous double doors. Without prompting, the group began describing a shared sense of heaviness and some were even feeling a little short of breath. We entered the room and the rest of the group expressed in no uncertain terms their disdain for the warehouse. Some of the groups have described seeing the image of a young man who appears in the warehouse, and all of them agree that the energy is very negative and they are afraid. Comparing notes with Patrick, it seems his impressions of the warehouse concur with those of the rest of the group.

Although we received no abnormal readings on any of the equipment, we definitely had enough direct hits to suggest the probability of paranormal activity. It would be very difficult to determine the source of the activity, given the wide range of reports and the lack of information about the land upon which the antique mall is built. Couple that with the personal belongings of incalculable amounts of people, many of who have passed away, and you have a recipe for the unexplained....

Patrick's Journal...

Driving down 22nd Street in Tucson, you wouldn't look at this antique mall and think of a haunted place. You might think you'd like to stop next door for some doughnuts after your day of shopping, but probably not that you may encounter some manner of paranormal activity. Entering the place, however, will cure you of this misconception almost immediately...as the large sales floor practically radiates with activity.

My route through the store was a bit meandering and haphazard, certainly more so than past investigations. I started down a row of booths and moved toward the back, almost immediately encountering a feeling of butterflies in my stomach and a weighty, heavy feeling in the air, as if it were pressing down on me. A brief distraction diverted me from the path Katie and Mikal were on, which turned out to be fortuitous, as you will see later. These feelings continued as I got closer to the back of the store, culminating in a very strong sense of not being alone in a back room that housed furniture. Upon entering this back room, I was struck with a sense of someone following right behind me and the air seemed to carry a dense, heavy feeling that made it difficult to breathe. (I have to pause to mention that when things are this profound this early in a walk-through, I am immediately skeptical of the feelings as it may just be my own subconscious justifying my presence there in the first place. In any investigation, you have to listen to your feelings and impressions, but also keep them in perspective.)

From this back room I made my way a little farther along the back wall where I found a set of double doors with the word *IN* written on it. I wasn't entirely sure at this point which areas we had access to, so I didn't go in. Instead, I doubled back and entered the annexed area of the building and made a circuit around the dim room. While in this area, the feeling of butterflies and that feeling of weight I had experienced earlier persisted. I heard footsteps above me and realized that the off-limits upstairs were actually on-limits, so I made my way up there where Mikal and Katie were already taking pictures and walking around.

This upstairs area hasn't been in use for two years, so the entire upstairs is empty save for some tables and chairs and, oddly, a small Christmas tree. The lighting was dim up there and the empty booths gave it a creepy feeling. Particularly... booth 52 seemed to draw such attention that I made note of filming the number. The weighty feeling and ever-present butterflies continued on this floor. It could have been the somewhat bizarre look of the empty rows or the increasing lack of light, but it really felt creepy up there—not a place I would want to hang out in by myself given a choice.

Moving back down the stairs, I continued my previous route along the back wall. At a particular point, almost dividing the store in half and very near to the previously mentioned double doors, all the weight, butterflies and shortness of breath dropped away. It was like walking around in a musty basement clogged with dust and then emerging into the open air. While on the west end of the store, I felt completely normal, no butterflies or other such feeling. In fact I found myself somewhat distracted by the items around me until I remembered we were there to investigate paranormal activity and not to shop. Still, there is a lot of cool stuff to look at so in the absence of the heebie-jeebies, I found myself distracted.

After doing a full circuit through the rows of booths, I found myself approaching the Mason-Dixon line of activity, and again was met with a heavy weight in the air and butterflies. Again my breathing became labored. At this meridian, Katie and Mikal were experiencing an anomaly with the digital camera that I wasn't picking up on my video camera. A quick recon of the area showed that the column they were getting was coming from some of the overhead light fixtures.

Happening upon Paul, the owner, I asked if we could go back through the double doors. He said we could and showed us through, turning on the lights. If the feelings of a presence and of butterflies, heaviness and shortness of breath were present before, they became absolutely palpable in this back area. The room stretches the length of the non-annexed main room and shares a wall with the furniture room that I mentioned earlier—a room I would not have encountered without the earlier distraction that separated me from the group. In this room, I felt a growing sense of a presence, specifically to the east end closest to the aforementioned room. As I moved back in that direction, the feeling grew more intense.

Upon finishing the walk-through we were taken around to different areas of the store where activity had been reported. Judy, Kathy, and Judy's daughter Gina, all of who have experienced activity in the store, led the way. Our first destination was the upstairs area, which as you know from the description section saw quite a share of activity. Hearing the story of the clacking picture in booth 52, Katie agreed that she had noted a strange feeling in that booth as well.

We crossed back into the main hall and were shown some booths in the area of the store where I had felt no activity, and were told of some happenings following the deaths of the booths' dealers. This activity was specific to the items at that booth and it seemed to be consistent with my abject lack of any feeling I had in the area. Again, I was not sure the authenticity of my feelings at all at this point. I knew the feelings were consistent and fairly strong, but nothing verified...yet.

Kathy asked if any of us felt anything in the back room beyond the double doors, and I said that I did and asked specifically to go back there. The ladies nodded and agreed it would be worth our time. As we were walking towards the back, they talked amongst themselves saying, "Do you feel it? It's getting heavier..." At that point I had not mentioned anything about my impressions or feelings, so I was surprised to hear my own vocabulary for what I was feeling repeated back to me. I mentioned what I had been feeling and everyone seemed to agree that it was what they had all felt as well.

Getting back into the warehouse area again, the feelings I had experienced before seemed to intensify, even as our guides said they felt the same thing. It's possible at this point that each of us were feeding off of our own imagination, but I am inclined to believe that was not the case as I hadn't mentioned my feelings beforehand, and they had scored a direct hit with previously reported activity.

Note was made of the breaker boxes in the back room and how entities may feed off the energy generated from them. I cannot speak to that, but it seemed as reasonable an explanation as any. Moving throughout the room, the feeling was always present and I found myself profoundly dizzy over time. In all the time I have done these sorts of investigation, these feelings rank among the strongest.

As is typical, I never saw anything or heard anything in the store. I didn't see anything moving or hear any ghostly noises. The feelings I had, however, were intense and tracked to the spot with reports by the employees of the store. Judy and Gina had many stories of seeing entities in the various areas including the back room, and were somewhat disappointed that such visual manifestations were not showing themselves. While it is profound when one sees a ghost, it is equally moving to feel the activity. Throughout the affected sections of the store, I certainly felt it. The number of hits built up too high to write off my feelings as an overactive imagination, and I feel very strongly that the store is the focal point of a great deal of activity. I can't speak to the visual sightings or poltergeist activity, but the correspondence of feelings with our guides is certainly compelling. The fact it is consistent in location also convinces me that this area is most certainly haunted. Given that these feelings were so present just walking around the place, this is a great location to visit for informal ghost-hunting. I was struck by just how palpable the feelings were, and it's a treasure trove for activity in terms of variety and intensity.

In terms of the casual ghost-hunter, 22nd Street Antiques is a great place to check out as it is large, offers a variety of activity in accessible areas, and there is a lot of stuff to look at. There is a wide selection of both items and activity to choose from and the ladies who work there seem very happy to share their stories. Besides, after all the shopping, stories and activity, there are also doughnuts.

Colossal Cave Mountain Park

www.colossalcave.com
16721 East Old Spanish Trail,
Vail, AZ 85641
(520) 647- 7275

Hours of Operation: Summer hours – (March 16 to September 15) Monday through Saturday, 8 a.m. to 6 p.m.; Sundays and holidays, 8 a.m. to 7 p.m. Winter hours – (September 16 to March 15) Monday through Saturday, 9 a.m. to 5 p.m.; Sundays and holidays, 9 a.m. to 6 p.m. Please visit their website or call them for admission cost and information.

Directions: From I-10, take exit 279 at Wentworth Road toward Vail Road. Turn left at East Colossal Cave Road/Wentworth Road. Continue on Colossal Cave Road, making a slight right to stay on the road. Follow signs to the park. Ample parking is available at both the ranch and the cave.

Intensity of paranormal activity: Moderate to high

Colossal Cave Mountain Park, located near Vail, is obviously best known for the cave itself, but it also includes La Posta Quemada Ranch as well as a sprawling campground. All three areas are open to the public for a fee, and all three hold interest for a would-be ghost-hunter.

Colossal Cave is unique among caves as it is what is known as a dry cave. Most caves are wet and thus still growing, but this one is essentially preserved and fixed. Given this, the cave allows for a level of interactivity that a wet cave could never provide. The touching of structure and even the introduction of air into wet caves can be disastrous to the formations as the acids and oils in one's hands can effectively halt the growth of the formations. Likewise, air tends to kill the structures by drying them out. This is especially troubling when one considers that it takes roughly 2,000 years per quarter of an inch of structure to grow. Disruption of that sort of growth should be inconceivable to anyone who loves nature. For this reason, Colossal Cave is a great find for those who can't help but to touch, and at the same time would rather not halt thousands of years' worth of a structure's progress.

The cave was discovered on January 15, 1879, by Solomon Lick, owner of the Mountain Springs Hotel and Stage Station, which was not far from what would become La Posta Quemada Ranch. Frank Schmidt, who acquired mining rights to the land in which Colossal Cave was nestled, took over the cave in 1922. In the early days of his ownership, Schmidt led tours through the cave for twenty-five cents. For their two bits, the guests would get a rope and a lantern and followed Schmidt through a completely wild cave.

Eventually, in 1934, Schmidt turned the rights of the land over to the state, which allowed the cave to be given federal funds for its improvement and general taming. The Civilian Conservation Corps (CCC) moved into La Posta Quemada and used it as a staging ground for the installation of stairs, railings, lighting, and walkways. The CCC also built up its camp and several of these buildings still occupy the Ranch today.

The work on the cave continued until 1938 and the cave was closed, although Schmidt continued to do tours through the cave. Charles Daley, who acquired La Posta Quemada in 1934, continued to build up the area during this time, running as many as six hundred head of cattle through the ranch and using the surrounding area as grazing land. The campground came into existence around this time as well.

In 1944, Pima County leased the land from the State of Arizona, and Frank Schmidt was named supervisor, a position he held until he was eighty-four. The land changed hands again in 1956, and again in 1964, when sole ownership of the sub-lease shifted to Joe Maierhauser. Maierhauser retained owner-ship until his death in 2007.

A number of remarkable things have occurred at the cave and its adjoining lands that make up the Mountain Park over the years. La Posta Quemada, which appropriately means 'Burnt Station,' has seen many fires over the years. One such fire ul-timately took the life of Solomon Lick's daughter after a candle overturned and set fire to the Mountain Springs Hotel. Unsur-prisingly, reports of seeing a little girl at the ranch have been tendered by those who have lived and worked at the ranch... and continue to this day. The ranch found itself plagued with fires as late as 1965, proving the ranch's name is apt.

Colossal Cave itself has seen its own action. Aside from being a home to the Hohokam Indians, whose sudden disap-pearance led to their name, which means "those who vanish," the cave has also allegedly played host to a group of bandits. According to the story, a trio of bandits fled to the cave after a train robbery and evaded capture by going out a back way, known as the Bandit's Escape Route, an entrance to what is known as the wild parts of the cave. The posse pursuing them eventually shot two of the bandits and the third was sentenced to seven years in the Yuma Territorial Prison. Given the heat in Yuma and the prison's dirt floors, he probably would have preferred being gunned down. Despite his capture, however, none of the money was recovered. It has long been rumored that the bandits stashed the loot, which was a substantial amount, in the cave. One would think if there were treasure to be had it would have been unearthed by the CCC when they did their work on the cave, but given the fact that the tour route makes up only about a quarter of a mile of a two- to five-mile cave, anything is possible.

The Cave has also seen some attention from Hollywood, although it's been the sort of attention you tend to brush under the carpet as opposed to brag about. The most recent effort being a 1994 horror film starring popular television actress Suzanne Somers, "Seduced by Evil."

The Ghosts...

As far as paranormal activity is concerned, the cave is covered in Patrick's walk-through account, but the ranch and camp grounds have their share as well. The Ranch has been something of a hot spot over the years, and with many of the employees of the ranch residing on the premises, it provides a perfect backdrop to reports of paranormal activity. One such employee, Rick Dailey, a soft-spoken cowboy who has worked the ranch for many years, has reluctantly had his own run-ins with strange goings on at the ranch.

He recalls one Easter night sitting down to dinner with his wife and daughter, as the night outside was drenched with pouring rain. They heard the sound of a horse walking through the mud: "He was wearing Jingle-bob spurs, I could hear the clinking." Assuming it was one of the nearby cattle owners caught in the freezing rain, he asked his wife to make some coffee and waited for a knock on the front door and prepared to welcome his surely drenched friend. When the knock never came and the delay became uncomfortable, his thinking became more suspicious. "I went and got a gun and went out the back door."

As is often the case with this sort of story, he looked around the premises and could find no evidence that anyone had been there. Still unnerved the following morning, Rick went out to cut trail in hopes of finding out who the lunatic riding in the rain had been, but found nothing. There was no trace of any kind of a horse having been through the area at all. He went outside again in the daylight to look for footprints in the mud and there were none. "No one was there," he said. "It bothered me."

Among the varied tales of paranormal activity on the ranch is the widely reported sound of children playing in a nearby creek bed. Rick has also heard the sound of the children playing, and has found evidence that might suggest the events that led to the activity. While riding his horse through the creek bed, he recalls finding the rim of a light carriage. Continuing down the creek bed, he found another rim. A later trip down the same creek bed yielded even more compelling evidence: "I went back down the canyon and found the metal frame of the buggy where a tree had grown around it. They must have been in the buggy and gotten caught in a flash flood and drowned." A scenario that is certainly feasible in the unstable monsoon weather for which Tucson is notorious.

Even though these reports suggest events that occurred over a hundred years ago, that is still very recent compared to the other sightings that have been reported. Over the years Rick has had employees staying on the ranch that have reported their own strange stories. The first came from an employee who was staying in the old adobe building the CCC used for its office. In the night as he slept on the floor of the building, he heard noises that sent him running from the adobe house and straight to Rick's front door. "He said, 'You ain't gonna believe this, Rick. I was layin' in there sleepin' and someone was throwin' rocks at the building!'" The two of them inspected the premises for the source of the rock throwing, but found nothing amiss. Rick returned to his home, and the ranch hand, convinced he had been visited by a group of long deceased Apaches, slept in Rick's truck...never to stay in the adobe building again.

Another such story came from a second employee who slept on the property, this time in the ranch's barn. He found himself awakened in the night to a group of Native Americans in full headdresses, dancing and chanting in the corral. Like the employee before him, he rushed up to Rick's house and began his report with the familiar phrase, "You're not going to believe this, but..." Again, the corral was inspected and found to be completely without dancing and chanting Native Americans.

Back at the Ranch itself, other workers who live there have described a little girl in a yellow dress who seems to follow the family from location to location on the ranch. Regardless of which house the family is living in, the little girl finds her way in. Given the death of Solomon Lick's daughter on the property, it's possible this is her spirit or an impression of her on the area.

The Ranch's gift shop is not exempt from activity, either. Employees of the shop have reported footsteps coming up to the tables in front of the shop. This activity is similar to footsteps heard coming into the gift shop at the cave itself. The Ranch is certainly alive...even if all its inhabitants might not be.

As mentioned earlier, the campgrounds have some activity to speak of, although here it's a bit subtler. In the back of the campground, close to the back gate, beyond which the road connects with the ranch, a feeling of dread and uneasiness has been reported. There is nothing specific in this activity...it's just a feeling. Certainly the whole campground is not saddled with this feeling, but once you start getting back toward that gate, it's best to have someone with you.

It's no surprise that an area that has been constantly occupied would have myriad activity. Colossal Cave Mountain Park as a whole has seen its share of history, and history has its way of leaving its mark. In this case that mark is a wide and varied collection of paranormal activity. When in the Tucson area, Colossal Cave Mountain Park is a must see not just for the paranormal but also a great day of nature, history, and fun.

Katie's Journal...

The park is divided into two sections, La Posta Quemada Ranch and Colossal Cave. Because our investigation focused on the cave, this account is a little different than the other locations listed in the book. There is a great deal of activity in the entire park and I would be remiss in my duties as an investigator and enthusiast of the paranormal if I did not include information pertaining to the ranch as well as the cave, even if I have no personal experience to use as a basis of comparison. The information regarding the ranch is made up of first-hand accounts of those who live and work there, and it definitely supports the possibility of paranormal activity.

We arrived at La Posta Quemada Ranch late in the afternoon and were greeted by our guide, Sandy Getts, with a very enthusiastic, "I'm a full believer in ghosts!" That immediately charged my anticipation. I was already feeling the buzz of the surroundings, in part due to the abundance of indigenous bees, but mostly because of the feeling of entering an area filled with history and activity. The ranch is located in a lush valley far off the beaten path and seemingly un-phased by technology. Certainly, the ranch enjoys modern advances, but at no time does it compromise its historic integrity.

It seems that no part of this park is without some manner of paranormal activity. From our meeting point at the gift shop, Sandy recalled several occasions of hearing the distinct sound of footsteps crunching in the gravel that leads to the patio, only to find no one there. She also recounted the tale of a co-worker who had at least one experience with a decidedly uncooperative radio that would turn itself on and off. Across the courtyard from the gift shop is the research library, run by librarian and photo archivist, Sharon Hunt. The library is a wealth of information dedicated exclusively to the park, which is a clear indication of exactly how much history has taken place on the ranch and at the cave.

Many of the employees of the ranch also live on the premises, giving a perfect backdrop to reports of paranormal activity. We were introduced to one such employee – Sarah – who started the interview with, "So, you wanna hear about our little girl in the yellow dress?" She went on to explain that her children and all of her nephews have reported seeing a young girl, roughly aged 8 or 9, wearing a yellow dress. This description matches the reports of the daughter of Solomon Lick, who died as the result of a fire on the premises over a century ago. The image of the young girl is seen in several parts of the ranch, as well as inside their home. Although Sarah reports no instances of mean-spirited mischief from the young spirit, her presence has been alarming enough to keep the visits from her nephews to a minimum, stating simply, "They won't stay here anymore."

Although we did not have the opportunity to experience the activity on the ranch first-hand, it is obvious in speaking to its residents that the activity is very real and rather frequent. Recalling one astute visitor's observation, Rick sums it up rather succinctly:

"He said, 'The valley is full of unsettled spirits.' I think he was right."

The entrance to the cave is a heavy, clanking wrought iron gate that brings to mind images of some subterraneous kingdom in which you might expect to find fairies and trolls and the like. While you may not actually see those creatures, you are definitely entering another world inside the cave.

We began the descent of the 363 steps, meandering carefully down the precarious path. The lighting is low and focused on the amazing stalactite formations that are absolutely breathtaking. As I took in the amazing scenery, I had absolutely no knowledge of the paranormal activity that had been reported...just that there had, in fact, been numerous reports. Under normal circumstances, there is a tour guide leading groups of people through each individual section of the cave. However, for our purposes, we were allowed to roam about freely and take the necessary readings and photographs, partly because of our need to have a little breathing room for research. It also helped that Patrick had actually spent a couple of years leading tours through the cave. On our way to the bottom, we picked up some unusual EMF readings, but I honestly had a hard time noticing any sensations other than the burning of my calves and thighs. I had not had any of my usual lightheaded, dizzy, kicked-in-the-gut symptoms that I associate with paranormal activity. When we reached the bottom, I walked towards a small staircase accessing a part of the cave that is off-limits. Although I could not enter that part of the cave, I could look over the gate and see a small part of its entrance. In that instant, I felt my internal ghost switch click into the "on" position and I was certain that someone was staring back at me. I had almost instant validation of my feelings when, as I reached for my camera, Patrick turned back around to me and said, "Get a picture of that, will you?"

After being instructed by Patrick to take a picture, Katie captured this orb.

We continued to walk down the path towards an area that contained some glass cases filled with different artifacts and memorabilia. It was in this part of the cave that I started to get the familiar dizzy sensation and had the overwhelming sense that I was being followed. Making note of that, we pressed on and began our return trip to the top of the cave. We bypassed the normal path by cutting through an off-limits passage that is affectionately known as the 'Phantom Staircase.' Names can certainly be misleading, but in this case I would have to agree that there might be a very good reason for the moniker. Stepping onto the staircase, I became so lightheaded that I could barely walk without grasping the handrail, and it felt like an unseen hand had a firm grip around my solar plexus. In my own defense, it should be noted that I am definitely not SO out of shape that I would be waylaid by a set of stairs, and I made it a priority to stay well hydrated. The EMF meter maintained a solid 10 reading, which definitely supported the theory that there was some really strong energy hanging around the Phantom Staircase.

We made it back to the entrance of the cave without further incident. Since Patrick had worked there for so long and already had full disclosure, the interview portion of the investigation was really just me showing him my notes and him saying "Yep" to all of the areas that turned out to be direct hits. In this case, the hits won by a landslide. Particularly interesting are the frequent reports of activity in all three of the areas where I had the strongest EMF readings and sensations.

Patrick's Journal...

For my part, the cave portion of the investigation wasn't business as usual if only because I spent two years as a tour guide there and any experiences I may have had on the walk-through were certainly tainted. As it was, I just served as a cameraman on the trip, going through the normal routine of videotaping our progress but not really taking part in the investigation. This particular trip was Katie's show as far as that was concerned, but I had many experiences during my time working there and have heard of many more. The retelling doesn't seem nearly as prolific as my experiences were, however, as the same things would happen over and over again. So when I say that I had many experiences, I am referring to the overall number and not the variety. It should be noted, as she described in her section, that Katie did replicate some of my experiences from the past.

When I first started working at the cave, the manager at the time told me of some of the activity that went on. She claimed that after about a month of working there, once the cave got used to you, it would start *TALKING* to you. While I thought that was strange, I more or less dismissed it as some new hire razzing and didn't give it much thought. I heard a little more when I was shown through the cave on those first days and we got to a location off of the Drapery Room called the Phantom Staircase. This area is blocked off now and is not included on the tour, but it bypasses the area called the Hallway of Time and goes straight down to the living room. Upon asking why it was called the Phantom Staircase, I was told that people had experienced some strange things on it, but I didn't get much other detail.

Eventually, after I had been there several weeks, I was in the cave by myself and decided to check out the Phantom Staircase. I walked down about halfway and stood for a moment, clicking my flashlight off and standing in the dark. I was alone in the cave at this point, but I started to hear voices whispering all around me. It was my name. Apparently this is what my manager meant when she said the cave would *talk* to you. Over the rest of my stay, I found that would happen often when I was by myself, not only in the Phantom Staircase, although that is where it happened most frequently.

Another thing that would happen with a fair amount of regularity is what is known as a "ghost tour." The ghost tour occurs when a guide is leading a group of people through the cave, and hears the sound of another tour going on in a room ahead of (or behind) said group. This is a bit tricky to authenticate given that throughout the course of the day there are multiple tours in the cave at the same time, so it is natural to assume that the ghost tour is simply another tour.

That explanation is all well and good for the middle of the day, since logic and safety dictate that you can't leave your charges to fend for themselves while you are playing ghost buster. It's a different matter altogether when it happens first thing in the morning or late at night. Those are the times — when you knew there was no one else in the cave with you — that really freak a person out. I recall a particular instance in which I was leading the first tour of the day into the cave. I had actually unlocked the gate myself and I knew for certain that there were no other tours in the cave at that time. As I stood at the end of the Hallway of Time, waiting for the rest of my group to catch up before continuing down the long staircase to the Living Room, I heard the familiar sound of another tour...in the Living Room. Now, we were the first people in the cave and the sounds were coming from a room we hadn't gotten to yet. It could be argued that because the Phantom Staircase connected the Drapery and Living rooms the sound could be carried through the staircase from the Drapery Room. However, I submit to you that my position on the stairs put me within arms reach of the passage leading back into the Drapery Room, so I would have been hearing it from both locations. The sound was definitely coming from the Living Room. I asked the members of the tour closest to me if they heard the sounds and they confirmed what I had heard — the sound of another tour guide talking to his group, and the group responding with laughter.

Acting on impulse, I briefly stopped my tour group to investigate the sounds. I moved down the stairs as quickly as I could without taking a header, and upon reaching the bottom of the stairs, the sounds I had been hearing stopped completely, and I found the room empty. I stood for a moment listening for any movement ahead of me and found there was none. I moved back up to rejoin my group, and the tour resumed uneventfully — no trace of the ghost tour anywhere.

Another morning, after unlocking the cave gate, I walked through the entrance and thought I saw someone standing to my left. Based on the location where I saw the figure, it would have had to have been hovering, as it was in a place where there was no footing. I shrugged it off as nothing more than too late a night and too early a morning (and perhaps too large a handful of chocolate-covered espresso beans) and went to my normal spot to begin the tour.

As I got there, I heard the sound of a soda can hitting the ground. Normally, that would not be considered paranormal in origin, but in this case it was very unusual. The front room of the cave consists of a stairway leading down and a platform (upon which I was standing) to the left, used by the tour guides during the opening spiel, allowing the guests' eyes to adjust to the dim light. The rear of the platform drops off a few feet from the walkway and behind the whole structure is a passage to a part of the cave known as the Ladder Route (a part of the cave that is not accessible during the course of a normal tour). I didn't want to slow the flow of my tour so as not to forget my place in my particular comedy routine, so I waited until after the tour was over to investigate the noise. It was a soda can, lying in that first passage to the Ladder Route. From where I found the can, it would had to have fallen from at least ten feet off the ground, and there is no reason whatsoever for a can to be discarded on a structure that no one could ever climb. I found it odd. I also found it annoying as that sort of business shouldn't be in the cave anyway.

Trips into the Ladder Route area were never my favorite either. Anytime I have been back there, I have always felt like someone was walking behind me. We went to that area on our walk-through, but I can't speak to the feeling because this time someone literally was walking right behind me. But that whole area has always felt very creepy to me. Unfortunately, that area is not on the normal tour; however, special arrangements can be made to go on that route at particular times. Check with the management for this, as policies may change between this writing and your reading.

Throughout the course of my time there I heard many stories of other strange things happening in the cave, with varying degrees of veracity. I hesitate to mention them here as they are not particularly substantiated, but they ranged the gamut from a guide doing clean up in the cave being beckoned to the back of the Hallway of Time by a man dressed as a cowboy who vanished, to a guide who claimed his shoelaces untied themselves in the Drapery Room in front of a tour full of people. Again, these are just stories I heard and may or may not hold any water at all, but if you take the Candle Tour, in which the lights are turned off and everyone sees by candle, you are likely to hear several ghost stories as those tours tend to focus on the history rather than the geology.

As far as the gift shop is concerned, the people I spoke to who work there now said they have never had anything strange go on, but when I was there I had several experiences around that area as well. Like the cave itself, there wasn't a wide variety of activity but there was a lot of it. I found when closing up at night, that if you walk in the area between the mountain and the gift shop, you could hear music coming from inside the gift shop. The people inside the gift shop hear nothing. At the time of my employment, I heard many stories of coworkers hearing said music. I am not certain if this still goes on as no one I spoke to during my visit had heard anything about it.

Another bit of gift shop activity that I found fairly disconcerting would also happen at night while closing. Standing in the front of the gift shop by the counter, I heard on several occasions footsteps walking into the shop. The first time it happened, I was with another employee and we both turned and said hello to no one at all. The footsteps sounded heavy, as if they were made by boots and tended to move along at a decent clip. When you are standing right there, it sounds like someone is about to run into you — turning to find no one tends to make you a little more reticent about closing up at night by yourself.

Moving back behind the gift shop into an area the general public cannot go, you'll find a two-story office building. In years past the ground floor was used as an apartment, but now it serves as storage. This building has seen its share of activity, including a fairly well-known story involving cave owner Joe Maierhauser. Between the Frank Schmidt years and the Maierhauser years, the cave had been owned by another party for a short time who didn't take particularly good care of the cave, leaving it to fall into disrepair. Shortly after Joe took over, he was in his office on the second floor and his unoccupied rocking chair began rocking on its own. Joe, believing this to be the spirit of Frank Schmidt, told the ghost, "Don't worry, we will get it clean and fixed again," and the chair abruptly stopped moving. Smelling pipe smoke around the area also tends to bolster the opinion that Frank is still knocking about watching over things.

There are many stories that I have heard over the years of various activity around the cave. Some I have experienced and some I have not. A visit to Colossal Cave doesn't guarantee paranormal activity, although you will have a lot of fun, learn a lot, and get some exercise. The cave is a wonderful place to visit, and my fondness for it places the years I spent there as some of my happiest. It is great fun and also has the added bonus of a possible brush with the paranormal. As with anything, you have to pay close attention to your feelings and understand that sometimes little feelings can translate into big hits. The cave is exceedingly safe; however, while paying attention to your feelings, you should also make sure you watch out for low-hanging rock fixtures as you could be knocked unconscious and fall over the railing. As I would tell my tour groups at the time, "That would be bad."

FOX THEATRE

www.foxtucsontheatre.org
17 Congress Street, Tucson, AZ 85701
(520) 624-1515

Hours of Operation: Please visit their website for upcoming events

Directions: From I-10, take exit 258 at Broadway/Congress. Continue east and you will see the marquis for the theatre on your left. Please note that, due to the possibility of construction on I-10, an alternate route may be necessary. If you are planning a visit from outside of Tucson, call the theatre for the best directions. Street parking is available within walking distance of the theatre. Please visit their website to download a map of the best parking areas.

Intensity of paranormal activity: Low to moderate

Located in downtown Tucson, Fox Theatre originally opened its doors on April 11, 1930. Its arrival heralded a new age of entertainment, bringing "moving pictures" to this small community and, with them, a taste of big city life. The brilliance of the flashing marquee beckoned, and every special occasion either began or ended with a stop at the Fox. The theatre thrived for several decades, each generation ceremoniously passing the keys to this landmark onto the next with the expectation that it could never be upstaged or replaced. Everyone's happiest memories should include Fox Theatre.

Sadly, this was not to be. By 1974, technology had far surpassed the capabilities of Fox Theatre and it was forced to close its doors. This matriarch of moviedom had seen its last audience, and with no more fanfare than the sound of a turning deadbolt, an entire era was gone. The theatre sat vacant for the next three decades, her once majestic presence rapidly deteriorating at the hands of vandals and vagrants.

In the early part of 2000, the building was purchased by the non-profit Fox Tucson Theatre Foundation, and for the next six years, every square inch of the theatre received a long overdue restoration. Like the kiss that awoke Sleeping Beauty, this project has given Fox Theatre renewed life and restored purpose.

The Ghosts...

Not much is known about who or what haunts Fox Theatre, although most people involved with the daily operations suggest it may be the spirit of a former employee, reluctant to leave his post and risk creating any disturbance to his beloved Fox. There has also been at least one sighting of a shadowy figure, which appeared to be dressed in attire reminiscent of the 1930s. Most commonly reported is the feeling of being watched, felt mostly by the female associates.

Katie's Journal...

From the moment we stepped into the theatre, I felt a little like a pair of worn brown shoes paired with a crisp black tuxedo. The theatre is stunning, and I felt woefully underdressed. We began our walk-through a little differently than most, with a guided tour led by Herb Stratford, General Manager. Rarely do we get treated to such a thorough, behind-the-scenes look at any of our investigation sites, let alone one of such historic significance.

The main lobby is immediately accessible from Congress Street, and it is the obvious starting point of the walk-through. From the outside, it is hard to imagine that just on the other side of the main entrance is 30,000 square feet spread over three levels of theatre. Walking through those doors is another story. The lobby is massive, and practically begs you to imagine starlets with bright red lips wearing sequined gowns, draped from the arms of well-dressed movie moguls with a penchant for pinstripes and fine cigars. Instantly, this building is alive.

The theatre has a lobby on all three levels. The uppermost lobby has the added bonus of an entire wall dedicated to memorabilia donated to the theatre or uncovered during renovation, including several popcorn boxes and an old usher's uniform. Even the glass display cases are true to the era, having been recovered from salvage at a nearby jewelry store and restored to their original 1920s glory.

Making our way past a portrait of one of the building's original owners, Mr. Stratford assured us the eyes of the painting would not follow us. We laughed, but I soon found myself wondering if that was true. The next set of doors led us to the balcony, and our first glimpse of the actual theatre. It was not unlike the scene in "The Wizard of Oz" where Dorothy opens her front door after landing, and the scene changes from black and white to technicolor. Honestly, the English language lacks the words that give proper brevity and inflection to the opulence and grandeur of this theatre.

After my initial reaction, my attention was immediately drawn to the stage. For the first time since I entered the building, I had the feeling that something was there. It was not menacing, just watching us from the stage. A snap of the digital camera revealed a nice, solid orb in the exact location that drew my attention, and gave me just a few goosebumps on the back of my neck.

As we passed through the balcony section on our way to the projection room, I was fascinated to learn that in its heyday, this theatre was host to many movie premiers and has been visited by countless early movie stars. John Wayne was a regular, routinely retreating to his favorite loveseat in the balcony, and writer/director Sam Peckinpah used the theatre to view dailies of his films. Knowing that the theatre was restored using actual photos and recovered samples of the original interior, it becomes very easy to imagine yourself sitting alongside these Hollywood icons.

Once inside the projection room, we learned that due to its architectural design, it has remained virtually unchanged since the restoration. The equipment has been updated and there was some slight revision to its appearance, but for the most part, it is the same projection room from the 1930s. It was in this projection room earlier in the day that Mike, the projectionist, had his own encounter with the ghost.

An orb waits for coming attractions at the Fox Theatre.

Describing a ball of tape that sits on his desk (used for attaching film to reels), he said that it started "crinkling as if someone were touching it." Unnerved, but not scared, he loudly (and somewhat sarcastically) invited the mischievous visitor to play with the ball. It was then that the ball rolled to the opposite side of the desk, and then rolled back to where it had begun.

Although the occurrences happen randomly, there is some predictability to the nature of the activity. Often, the computerized equipment will have settings changed or deleted, and reels of film are mysteriously moved. Access to this secured area is very limited, and entry requires a key. This has led the staff to the idea that perhaps a former employee, or someone else, is visiting them with a personal connection to the theatre.

Reportedly, activity is not limited to the projection room. Mr. Stratford's associate Jennifer describes it:

"I get a vibe all the time, like somebody is watching me... right behind me."

Although Jennifer's feeling intensifies on a particular staircase in the building, she does recall a time she was alone beneath the stage, cleaning the mirrors in a dressing room. "I had just finished cleaning the water spots off of the mirror, but when I went back a few minutes later, the spots were back!"

If there is a place in Arizona that should be haunted, it would certainly be Fox Theatre. Its rich and colorful history has woven a tapestry that has encompassed many lifetimes, providing a backdrop to mark the happy occasions of many generations.

"People were proposed to here, people met their spouses here, had their first job here," Mr. Stratford acknowledges. "There are so many happy memories at the Fox, that if there's a spirit or a sense of that, it is because of all the laughs and all the good times that have happened."

I couldn't agree more.

Patrick's Journal...

Typically, when one thinks of a haunted place it immediately conjures up images of something dark and creepy or, at the very least, something a bit unsettling. Upon entering the Fox Theatre in downtown Tucson, those images are quickly dispelled as you are greeted with a friendly, open, and colorful environment. As we started our walk-through I was struck by the theatre's general feeling of comfort. Not to gush or get ahead of myself, but as a film and theater buff, this was one of the coolest places in which I have ever set foot.

The walk-through ran differently than the ones we normally do in that we all walked through together, guided by General Manager Herb Stratford. He took us all through the theatre, from the common areas to the places the general public would never see. From start to finish, the theatre was incredibly impressive and stands as a testament to the work, money, and love that went into its restoration.

We began in some of the lower lobby areas and continued into the areas below where the ductwork and air conditioning units are housed. These areas, like the rest of the theatre, were once used as a squat for the homeless, whose rivalrous groups marked their respective living areas with things like jackets hanging on the walls (like some manner of underground scarecrow) to fend off potential looters. Even down under the theatre the feeling wasn't scary or oppressive or otherwise off-putting.

We moved back up into the balcony of the theatre. The view in the room was staggering. The carpets and upholstery have been restored to match the original decor, the light fixtures have similarly been replicated, and the ceiling is a beautiful example of 1930s era southwestern design. Even the theatre's ventilation is hidden in a lattice-like design around the ceiling, making it look like a part of the architecture and obscuring its true purpose. This design device illustrates the elegance of the building, allowing for nothing as garish as crude vent panels to sully the structure's beauty.

Next we moved up to the projection booth, which was the first location to see regular paranormal activity. Earlier in the day, a large ball of tape on the cutting table had begun to vibrate. The projectionist working at the time said aloud, "If you are going to play with it, then play with it!" In answer, the ball rolled to one side of the table and promptly rolled back. Certainly not normal behavior for your average tape ball, although to be fair, he did give it the go ahead. From an investigator's standpoint, a ball of tape rolling down the table really doesn't warrant much attention beyond the odd coincidence of when it happened. The ball of tape subsequently rolling back, however, certainly gives one pause.

According to the projectionist, activity is not at all uncommon in the projection room, although not normally so profound as a ball of tape moving independent of any motivation. Machines in the room will have their dials and settings changed and other such meddling tends to go on. Nothing really major happens, just little things from time to time — which is more often than not how it goes.

Another orb – possibly cueing up the equipment – peers out of the projection room of the Fox Theatre (2nd window from left).

From the projection booth, we were shown another area under the booth that had at one time been a bathroom but more recently served as a hiding place for liquor bottles and a repository of refuse from the 1930s such as candy wrappers and other packaging of the time. Again, one gets a true sense of the staggering activity and history the theatre had experienced and had defied the odds in its own preservation.

From there we proceeded into the under stage and backstage areas. The under stage houses the dressing rooms, organ pumps, and a green room for the entertainers who play the venue. Some of these areas were not part of the original structure, but have been co-opted in the restoration process to provide amenities the original theatre didn't offer. The dressing rooms in this area are well tended and have also offered some disturbances of their own. Again, the activity here seems to be mischevious such as water spots reappearing once the mirrors have been washed. Some workers have reported feeling a presence in these under stage areas, as if they are being followed as well.

Moving backstage, we went on the stage itself to look out at the theatre from that vantage. As breathtaking as the view is from the balcony, the view from stage threatens to buckle the knees. I can only imagine the rush of performing on that stage for over a thousand people.

After the tour we talked to Herb, and his colleague Jennifer, more about the reported activity. Jennifer herself has experienced a feeling of being followed or generally not being alone on many occasions. Typically, this occurs when she is alone or with a small group and continues today, although less frequently now than during the restoration period. Further, the cleaning crew has reported seeing a ghostly figure when only four of them were there on at least one occasion.

The general consensus is that whatever is haunting the place is a former crewmember as no sightings or activity have ever been reported during a show. Patrons have not reported any activity at all, lending more credence to the theory...as a crewmember would be as invisible as possible during a performance.

Again, it must be noted that in just about every case, the feeling of the theatre is not at all creepy or foreboding. Whatever may or may not be there is in no way malevolent. It's a good example of the fact that not all activity has to be spooky or scary or in any way negative. A place like this has seen an abundance of happiness and good times as entertainment has cheered the lives of its patrons for many years. When you think about it, given the joy and love of the place, why would anyone want to leave?

There seems to be a variety of activity going on in the theatre from what may be an apparition to haunting phenomena. In terms of a haunting, an event doesn't have to be traumatic to leave an imprint on the place, just emotionally intense. Certainly joy and elation qualify, so it's not a major leap to assume that perhaps those good times stuck around.

As it is a working theatre, a walk-through of the place is not likely. If you plan to visit the Fox, your best bet would be to take in a show. In the spirit of completeness and also an overwhelming desire to see a movie there for my birthday, we went back after our investigation to see "The Big Lebowski," a treat for sure.

Consistent with reports, nothing paranormal happened while we watched the film, although a trip to the concession area left me with a buzzing in my stomach that was more excitement than anything. The experience of seeing a film there is great and if you show up early you can walk around a little and get a feel of the place. I absolutely enjoyed every moment of the movie-going experience as well as the walk-through experience.

Fox Theatre is grand in every sense of the word. It is large and welcoming and is just a comfortable place to see a movie or show. That it is haunted further adds to the allure. Its activity is subtle and is indicative of the way most haunted places truly are. Hollywood has conditioned people to believe that it's all flash and terror, so it is strangely ironic that an epic portal to Hollywood such as this would demonstrate the reality of the paranormal. It doesn't have to be big and in your face, and most of the time it's not. That the stories from the Fox are so grounded and consistent lends credibility to the tales. While on the walk-through I didn't feel anything strange or get any strong impressions one way or the other, but the nature of the reported activity suggests strongly that said reports are true. If absolutely nothing else, the Fox is a wonderful venue and should be a mandatory stop on any Tucson visit, haunted or not.

THE HOTEL CONGRESS

311 East Congress Street,
Tucson, AZ 85701
(520) 622-8848
(800) 722-8848
www.hotelcongress.com

Hours of Operation: Hotel lobby is open and staffed twenty-four hours a day. Call the hotel for club hours.

Directions: From I-10, take exit 258 at Broadway/Congress east to 5th Avenue. Turn left and continue through the light. The hotel is on the right. Limited parking is available at the hotel. Additional parking is available next to the Rialto Theatre between Broadway and Congress at 4th Avenue.

Intensity of paranormal activity: Moderate to high

Built in 1919, the Hotel Congress was the perfect resting point for passengers traveling the Southern Pacific railway lines. Its southwestern design was the height of style, and the accommodations were considered nothing short of luxurious. An oasis in the desert, the Hotel Congress was a delight to travelers from as far away as the East Coast.

Besides being a popular destination for those en route to California, the Hotel Congress claims its spot in American history as the hideout for one of America's most notoriously untouchable gangsters — John Dillinger. After robbing numerous banks throughout the Midwest, resulting in the brutal deaths of several bystanders and at least one police officer, the gang stole away under the cloak of night to lay low in Tucson. They had hoped to put enough distance between themselves and their crime spree to allow the frenzy to die down while living the good life compliments of their ill-gotten fortune.

This was not to be. On January 22, 1934, a fire broke out in the basement of the hotel, tearing through the elevator shaft to the third floor, where Dillinger and his motley crew had been carefully guarding their stash of cash and weapons. Although they escaped the fire by way of aerial ladders, they overplayed their hand by generously tipping two firemen to retrieve their heavy luggage. It was these very firemen that later recognized Dillinger from an article in *True Detective* magazine, and after a very brief but non-violent stakeout, Dillinger was finally captured.

The Ghosts...

Many guests and residents have come and gone since the Dillinger affair, and according to several legends, some hotel guests have remained long since "checking out." Many people have reported seeing a man in a vintage grey suit, believed to be known as "T. S." These witnesses have seen him peering from his window on the second floor...even when there was nobody occupying the room. Popular lore indicates that he may have been the victim of a gunfight over a card game.

T. S. is certainly not the only ghostly resident of the hotel. Joining him in his notoriety is a young Victorian lady who prefers to make her presence known by descending the grand staircase of the hotel, dressed in proper Victorian attire and smelling of delicate roses. Those who have been with her on the staircase have noted that the strong floral smell comes on suddenly and disappears as quickly. At the top of those stairs is room 242 — a room that was witness to the final moments of one unfortunate resident...whose untimely death was both sudden and tragic, and some believe the spirit still remains.

The most well-known and beloved ghost is that of Vince, a delightful gentleman who was a thirty-six-year resident of the hotel and also the hotel's handyman. Vince was very resourceful, and was known to use butter knives to tighten loose screws around the hotel. Vince apparently has a rather strong work ethic because since his passing in 2001, hotel staff members continue to report finding the butter knives that he is still leaving around the hotel.

Whether you are a budding paranormal investigator or an ultra hip urbanite, Hotel Congress is not to be missed. With its combination of vintage charm and modern nightlife, it is easy to see what keeps the guests coming back time and time again, alive or otherwise.

Katie's Journal...

We arrived at Hotel Congress later in the evening, half expecting a nice, quiet little haunted hotel where every creak of a floorboard could be heard and dis-embodied footsteps and voices were palpable. We were mistaken. The Hotel Congress is one of the hippest hot spots in the newly revitalized downtown Tucson, juxtaposing its 1930s-era southwestern art deco with the swinging vibe of the very nocturnal urban social scene.

The three of us checked into Room 242 and set up our equipment. In retrospect, it seems odd to me that all of us are native Tucsonans (for the most part) and yet none of us had any knowledge of any of the paranormal activity...just that the hotel is reputed to be haunted. Immediately, I noticed that I could not get any stable read on the EMF detector, especially in the area between the closet and the bed. We set the EMF detector on the dresser and just watched it for the next fifteen minutes. It would go from a zero reading to a five, back down to two, and then all the way up to ten. Then it would stop completely, but only for a minute, and then begin with another random set of readings. Honestly, if I didn't think I knew better, I would swear that it was some kind of Morse code message. I have been on a lot of investigations and I have never seen anything quite like that. It continued this way for the rest of the investigation. The room was devoid of any type of electronic devices, save for a ceiling fan, desk lamp, and an old-style radio, the latter two items being located on a desk on the opposite side of the room.

I left the EMF detector to its own devices, and Mikal took out the camera and started taking pictures. In one of the pictures, Patrick actually has a nice, solid orb sitting on his shoulder, which made me think, "Okay...maybe there is something to this." We did our walk-through of the entire second floor, noting a few spots that made me feel dizzy and lightheaded, but nothing terribly spectacular. At one point, as I was climbing the stairs, I definitely felt as though someone was following me, which, as I later found out, was not uncommon on the staircase, although it is usually accompanied by a strong smell of roses.

Returning to the room, we made another sweep with the EMF detector. I opened the closet door and checked the reading on the inside. The readings elevated near the grouping of hang-ers, literally focusing on one hanger in particular. I thought this was very strange. "Now why on EARTH would ONE HANGER be having such a high reading, Katie," I thought to myself, but shelved the issue without mentioning it to anyone. I would later find out that this was actually one of our biggest hits.

At this point, we decided to "go dark," if you will, and turned off all the lights. Even though we could not make the room com-pletely dark because of the neon streaming in through the blinds, we managed to make it dark — and still — enough to get some really strong impressions. We each took turns sitting in different parts of the room, making notes of what thoughts or feelings we had. One part of the room that we all completely, and strongly, agreed on was the bathroom. Easily the most efficiently compact bathroom I have ever visited, it was every bit as intense as it was tiny. I could not stay in there for very long because the minute I closed the door, I felt as though I was not alone, and it made me extremely anxious...if not frightened. Now, let me clarify, the rest of the group was less than ten feet away on the other side of a door that was not locked, and I was just as panicked as if I had been accidentally locked inside of a dark basement all alone. Mikal and Patrick felt exactly the same way. After we all took turns sitting in the bathroom, we vehemently agreed that the energy in the bathroom was very, very strong.

Although the strongest impressions I had were in the bathroom, they were certainly not the only ones that I experienced. Sitting on the floor by the closet, I felt goosebumps...as I heard the closet door creak, even though the door did not open. That was followed by an intense feeling that someone else had just suddenly come into the room. A later comparison with Patrick was significant because he noted a similar sensation while sitting on the bed. He mentioned that he felt someone had walked past me (from that closet area) and stopped at the foot of the bed.

The other noteworthy experience happened while I was sitting in the desk chair across the room from the bathroom. The lights were out, everyone was still, and I was still transfixed on the bathroom — convinced I was seeing shadows moving — when my chair moved as though something had bumped into it. I wasn't frightened by this, but I do recall saying, "Hey guys, my chair just moved...seriously."

Since the room we investigated had only a single bed (of course, other rooms in the hotel have more than one bed, but for our purposes we were more interested in the paranormal activity), Mikal and I left to allow Patrick to sleep the rest of the night in the room. We had already collected quite a bit of evidence to support the claims of paranormal activity, but we were still very curious to see if Patrick had any unusual experiences after we left. We were not disappointed.

I spoke with Patrick very early the next morning after he had gotten the rundown on the events that transpired in the room from staff. Given our experiences from the night before, I was not at all surprised to learn that someone had died in the bathroom. What makes the evidence more compelling is the manner in which they died — a gunshot wound, which left a hole in the adjacent closet wall...in the exact place where I received the enormous EMF reading. As far as I am concerned, that sealed the deal.

Let it be known that while the Hotel Congress lovingly embraces its ghosts, it is not something that should be taken lightly or irreverently. Those that are rumored to haunt the hotel were once very much alive and loved dearly. While visiting, please be respectful at all times and refrain from any activity that would dishonor their memory.

Patrick's Journal...

You never know what to expect when you walk into an investigation. Because it's best to go in blind so as to not taint your experience, you never know what activity you might encounter and how you might encounter it. If you keep this aspect of the investigation intact, you can have some very interesting and significant findings and it provides you an insight as to whether or not you are in tune with the paranormal. Sometimes you walk into a place and your instruments go crazy and there are really obvious things going on, but I find that more often than not, it's the little things that you would dismiss that tend to provide the most direct hits. If you show up and you get tons of readings, you might be so focused on the fact that the EMF detector is going crazy that you miss a small feeling in your stomach or in the back of your mind that is really "something." At Hotel Congress in Tucson, I found that this principle was definitely applicable.

From the moment we stepped into the cozy single room and got our equipment going, we noticed some very strong and anomalous readings from the EMF detector. It started going crazy around the closet, dresser, and bed, and there was no apparent reason why. Our checks for wiring in those areas or any manner of electrical equipment came up empty. Moving the detector around made it apparent that whatever was causing the readings was on the move; it was consistent to one area...but not the same spots in that area. We made a circuit around the room with the EMF, and the readings stayed in that general area.

Because of the strong EMF we took pictures of the room and found several pictures were coming up with orbs. These were not isolated in just one area, but seemed to be all over the room. Entering the bathroom, which is fairly small, I found myself feeling uneasy and not entirely alone. Fair enough, though, given there were three of us in the room.

After looking around our room, we conducted the standard walk-through of the hallway, stairs, and lounge area. After two circuits around the floor, I had feelings of dizziness at the top of the stairs and a distinct feeling of being followed at one point. Aside from those, there really didn't seem to be much going on out there.

An orb making its way up the stairs at Hotel Congress.

Back in our room we decided to turn the lights out and sit in the dark and see how things felt. The space in the room was somewhat limited so Katie laid on the bed, I sat in a chair by the window, and Mikal sat in the bathroom. I had the distinct impression that someone was standing near the closet and moving into the room. I would catch movement out of the corner of my eye and just generally feel a presence there. This continued until Mikal wanted to get out of the bathroom as he felt it was creepy, and I went in and sat on the toilet, closed the door, and turned out the lights. That lasted maybe three minutes before I had to get out of the room. I had a very distinct feeling of not being alone.

Over the course of the next hour or so, we all switched positions in the room. At one point, as I laid on the bed, Mikal asked if I had been whispering something. I told him that I had not been, and we shrugged off the whispering. Mikal and Katie packed up to go home and soon left me alone for the night.

My first order of business was to close the bathroom door because I just couldn't lay in the bed with it open. The door didn't close all the way, but it was close enough. I got in bed and tried to sleep.

Now, it can be kind of hard to sleep during overnight investigations. For me, a lot of it has to do with the general excitement of doing an investigation, and it's hard to shut my brain off long enough for sleep to get its foot in the door...that and the fact that the place is haunted. I've been doing this for a long time and have had many experiences, and it would seem that I wouldn't get frightened by staying in a haunted place, but the nature of the business dictates that no matter how many times you do it, you will be creeped out. I suspect that alone is why many people are interested in investigations in the first place.

In this case, I was uneasy about the feeling in the bathroom and was trying to just put it out of my mind to go to sleep. Then the bathroom door creaked open some more. Now, as I have already mentioned, the door didn't close all the way so it could just have been the wind or the door settling, but it had already opened to where it normally stayed and there were no great gusts of wind or anything. Again, it may have been nothing, but it added to my level of building unease.

Flipping to my other side, I gave it a try facing the bathroom. As I drifted off at this point I felt a pressure on my back as if someone had sat down on the side of the bed and was partially leaning on me. I reached back and loosened the covers so they wouldn't be so tight around me and almost immediately it happened again. I thought this was strange, but discarded it as I tried to sleep.

Eventually I slept and the rest of the night was uneventful. I woke up aware of having dreamt, but I hadn't written it down during the night, so whatever the dreams were they had escaped me. When you are doing overnight investigations, you always want to keep a notebook handy to jot down any dreams you might have, as often they can be as significant as anything you see or experience while awake. Sadly I didn't do this; lesson learned.

After showering and packing up, I went downstairs and spoke with the desk manager to see if we had any hits. As it turns out, a few of the things we didn't really put a lot of stock in seemed to be hits. The whispering Mikal heard is reported activity, as is the feeling of being touched in bed. That seemed to correspond with my feeling of someone sitting against my back.

More significant was the bathroom, which, as it turns out, was the spot where a former resident of the hotel was killed. This seemed to validate all of our uneasiness with — and the EMF readings surrounding — the bathroom. The closet shares a wall with the bathroom, so it's conceivable that the readings we were getting were related to the tragedy that occurred there.

Again, this is a good illustration of trusting even the smallest of impressions and feelings. Had some of these feelings been discarded, perhaps connections wouldn't have been made and experiences not replicated. It is very important to pay close attention to all feelings and impressions…as you never know what may turn out to be significant.

Hotel Congress is a fairly well-known location in Tucson. Its attached club is home to many live shows and regular theme nights. It's exciting and energetic as well as vintage and historical. This blend of the modern from its Internet café to its decidedly old-school flavor makes for an enjoyable stay overall even without any activity. The addition of paranormal goings on is an added bonus for the curious. It should be noted, however, that while you think the paranormal is cool, it is there because a person died, and it would serve you well to remember that the loss of life is not quaint or something to take lightly. With this in mind, the Hotel Congress is a great place to visit and to investigate with the utmost professionalism and decorum.

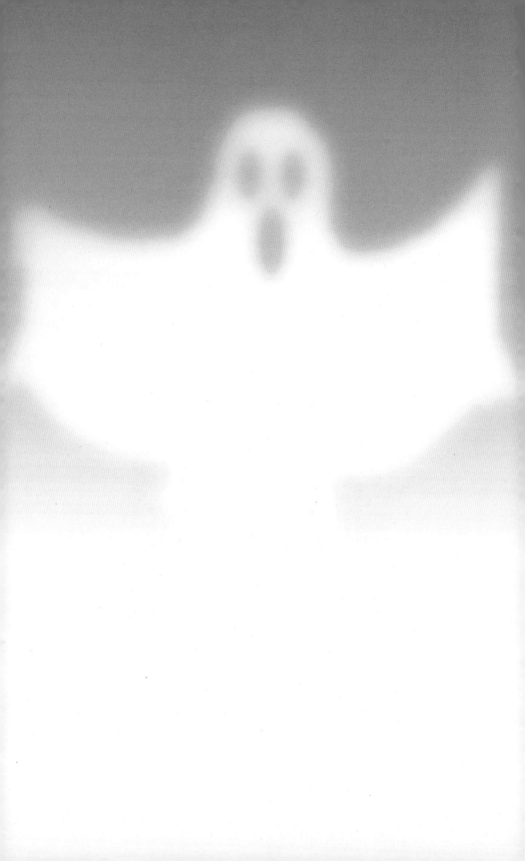

Section Three:
Tombstone

When a place is called "The Town Too Tough to Die," you have to expect that some of its former residents were just that.

Directions: From I-10 East, take exit 303 towards Benson/Douglas and follow the signs. Of course, the city itself is open year round, but you may want to consider planning a winter visit, as the summers in southern Arizona are rather brutal.

When you are writing a book about haunted places in Arizona and you begin talking to people, one thing you will never escape in the conversation is, "Have you gone to Tombstone?" More than just the subject of countless western movies, this town embraces the history of the state much more vigorously than any other. Allen Street in particular preserves the feel of the old west better than anywhere else in the state, and while the carriage rides and occasional mock gunfights take place amongst a glut of gift shops, you are not likely to find history preserved any better.

In Tombstone you can walk the same floorboards as legendary gunfighters and cowboys and dine in the same restaurants and buy mouse pads and t-shirts in the same shops they may have purchased their wares. Given the level of violence found in the place, it is no surprise that while you can tread the same steps left by the legendary figures, in some cases you can be treading those steps alongside them.

Founded in 1877 as a mining claim by Ed Schieffelin, Tombstone became something of a lightning rod for violence and 'Wild West' mayhem. Some of the most notorious figures of western history converged here...often with bloody consequences. Certainly the most famous event in Tombstone's history is the Fight at the O.K. Corral between the Earp Brothers, and the Clantons and McLaurys. This battle, which is the subject of some debate as to exactly how and where it happened, has become something of an archetypical Wild West moment, and has inspired a glut of movies and books. It also escalated already white-hot tensions between the Earp brothers and the Cowboys, America's first example of organized crime. The violence that ensued reached such fever pitch that President Chester A. Arthur actually threatened Arizona Territory with martial law. It's no wonder the place is so haunted...it's said that spirits walk the streets.

There are several places in the town that are said to be haunted, and we are going to touch on the most prominent here. This section is somewhat different than the others as Tombstone is not a place in which you can go and do formal investigations for the most part. It's a tourist town and the haunted places along Allen Street are all very accessible, but actually going in and disrupting business or doing overnight stays are often times not possible. This section will give you an idea of the places you can check out, if not have experiences yourself. When we went down, we found a mixed bag in terms of people willing to talk about the hauntings and ghost stories. In one case we were told that the stories the person had heard were all untrue. Not everyone believes in ghosts, obviously, and some people are reluctant to talk about them. That is fine, don't be pushy... just smile and thank them for their time. Further, not everyone is as interested in ghosts as we are, and when you are talking about a historical place where people deal in hard facts, you are going to run into people who aren't interested in ghosts at all. So, ask around, but don't expect everyone to be into talking about it.

Ghosts or no, Tombstone is enormously interesting, especially if your interest lies in early western history and the mystique surrounding gunslingers and cowboys, so it's well worth a visit even if you can't set up shop for a formal investigation. Being able to go to the spot where many of the west's bloodiest and most storied altercations occurred is not dull and there are many cool things to see. Besides, you never know what may happen while sitting in a cantina, walking around a corral, or even just walking down the street.

The locations listed below are not only filled with paranormal activity, but are also very conveniently located on, or within a short distance of, Tombstone's historic Allen Street.

BIG NOSE KATE'S

I'll start with Big Nose Kate's, because of all the locations in Tombstone, this is the one I have actually formally investigated. The results of the investigation are not mine to publish as it was one of the first I took part in with the Pima College group, but I can give you the broad strokes.

Big Nose Kate's was built in 1881 and known at the time as the Grand Hotel. It was a popular location in Tombstone with a guest list that reads like a who's who of the time. Its current name comes from Big Nose Kate, the girlfriend of Doc Holiday and Tombstone's first working girl. Other guests included

Doc Holiday himself, and the Earp brothers. The Clantons and McLaurys were guests the night before their fateful shootout with the aforementioned Earps at the O.K. Corral, which happened on the same date as the investigation with the Pima College group, more than a century earlier.

Aside from the actual bar and dining area, the saloon also boasts an upstairs area used by staff and a basement area that houses The Shaft, a gift-shop/clothing store that specializes in western attire. The Shaft also includes the former bedroom of the "Swamper," a custodian/amateur miner who spent his spare time looking for silver in a catacomb mine beneath town that he had managed to tap into. The shaft into this mine can still be seen in his bedroom, which is separated from the rest of the shop by prison-style bars.

An orb – possibly The Swamper – watches suspiciously as he guards his silver mine at Big Nose Kate's.

The décor in the saloon is vintage, much like many of the other historical buildings in Tombstone, and the bartenders and waitresses dress up in a like manner. The bartenders also tend to be fairly versed in history and local lore. Looking around you'll find large mirrors, paintings, and a pair of small balconies that currently house a TV and some posters.

During our investigation, we did a full walk-through and spent the night on the floor of the gift shop. This is not something the general public will be able to do, but by and large, the activity in the place takes place in common enough areas that it doesn't really matter. In particular, the Shaft has a definite vibe to it. There is a palpable feeling of not being alone, especially when near the Swamper's room. Indeed many people have reported seeing a figure walking around down there, and photographs have captured shapes, figures, and mist. I didn't see any of that personally, but I certainly didn't feel normal. When we went down for the purposes of this book, we did get an orb in the Swamper's room. It's a room with a dirt floor so it is entirely possible that this was from dust, however, we took several pictures of the room and none of the others had any orbs or dust so one would think that is significant. Again, the area around the Swamper's room is fairly creepy, orbs or no. Even when you are the only one down there, you feel like you aren't alone in the gift shop.

Coming down the stairs to the gift shop has its own surprises as well. The stairs spiral tightly and sometimes while walking down them people feel as if they are being tapped on the shoulder or getting hit with a rock kicked from the top floor. When I investigated, I felt and heard a dirt clod hit my shoulder. Of course, upon inspection, there were no remnants of any such clod nor was there anyone up there to have kicked it down the hole.

The area in the back, now used as a gallery and the location of the men's bathroom, also feels very strange and you feel very much not alone. Further along in that back area there is the staff staircase leading to the upper floor that has its share of activity. There are many stories of staff getting the impression that someone is walking behind them as they walk down these stairs. Some of these have gone so far as to describe the feeling of being pushed. The generally held belief is that all of this is attributable to the Swamper, who was very protective of his tunnel and his silver. After all, he did tunnel his way to a mine through the basement of the hotel himself. Of course, a place like this with as much history as it has could conceivably play host to other entities, but at the moment it appears that Swamper is the man.

Further, the balcony at one time had dummies of cowboys sitting up there playing cards — and the dummies used to get in the act. There is a story of a bartender coming in to work and seeing the heads of the dummies on the balcony turn to look at him. Needless to say, it was a short shift for him that day. I can't say if this is why the dummies are no longer there, but I would certainly not want to keep them around after they decided to turn and look at me.

Big Nose Kate's is a must visit in Tombstone. The food is great as is the atmosphere and there's been enough activity to allow for the possibility of an experience just visiting. Don't miss it.

CRYSTAL PALACE SALOON

Opening its doors on July 23, 1882 on the site of the burned down Golden Eagle Brewing Company, the Crystal Palace Saloon was a popular spot in Tombstone. It boasted honest gambling and tended to keep the violence of Tombstone outside its doors. Its top floor served as offices for Virgil Earp, the oldest Earp brother and Marshal of Tombstone, as well as Dr. George Goodfellow, a respected physician, and even the coroner Dr. H. M. Matthews. The Crystal Palace stood out amongst all the plentiful saloons in Tombstone and found its clientele among virtually every sort of person in the town. Some of them have reportedly decided to stick around.

Guests and employees have described not only seeing ghostly cowboys around the bar, but have seen things move and spin on their own. It's another place where you have a decent chance of having an experience.

NELLIE CASHMAN'S RESTAURANT

Formerly the Russ House, Nellie Cashman's Restaurant was converted to a restaurant in 1882. Nellie Cashman herself was an Irish immigrant who was enormously well loved and eventually came to be called the 'Angel of Tombstone' for her extensive good deeds. She was strongly religious and a gifted businesswoman. During her time in Tombstone, Cashman opened a grocery store and saloon in addition to the restaurant.

The restaurant and former hotel have its share of reported activity. We visited the restaurant and took some pictures, but did not do any kind of full investigation. We were told that activity not only occurred inside by the kitchen entrance, but also outside on the patio. Reportedly, this activity includes objects being moved and the lights turning on and off. Further, ghostly figures have been reportedly seen in the restaurant. None of our photos gave us any orbs or mist, and our brief time in the restaurant didn't yield any activity. Many of the reported happenings have occurred to customers, so it is possible that some activity may be observed while having a meal. The prices are reasonable and the food smelled awesome. Definitely a good bet to check out.

RED BUFFALO TRADING COMPANY

Formerly Campbell and Hatch's Billiards and Saloon, this is the site where Morgan Earp was shot on May 16, 1882 while playing pool with Bob Hatch. The shooting was in retaliation for the O.K. Corral. This event led to further retaliation by Wyatt Earp, who was present for his brother's death. The area is now a store with a wide variety of western items for purchase, and marks the exact spot of Morgan's death with a pool table and information regarding the killing. A flier also mentions that Morgan may still haunt the place.

Inquiries into the matter with the staff turned up little information, but allegedly a figure believed to be Morgan himself has been seen around the place. It is fairly cool to be able to go in and see where this happened, but you shouldn't expect to see too much by way of activity. Still, it is worth a look as there's quite a bit of cool merchandise and you never know what you may see.

SCHIEFFELIN HALL

Named for the founder of Tombstone, Schieffelin Hall was something of a cultural center for the town — playing host to operas and other such high-class events. The Hall served a bit higher-class clientele as well, and even saw the favor of national touring groups. It thrived for many years, but eventually became used only as a Masonic lodge. It is restored now and generally open to the public.

Sadly, our ill-fated trip to Tombstone saw it in the midst of construction so we weren't able to go in. Still, the Hall is an impressive figure standing large and noticeable even from Allen Street. The nature of the activity at Schieffelin Hall seems to be sounds. Many people have reported auditory activity coming from the building and some of the Masons have reported various sounds while holding their meetings.

These are the most well known haunted places in Tombstone, but I am confident in saying that they are not the only ones. When violence spills out on the streets and a Marshall can be murdered on the street or two groups of armed men can fight it out in a vacant lot behind a corral, you can expect there to be activity everywhere. For this reason, Tombstone as a town is not a bad bet when looking for places to check out for paranormal activity. You aren't likely able to stage a full-scale investigation, but you may get one or two good stories out of the townsfolk at various locations. You may even have some experiences of your own...if you are on the look out. When a place is called "The Town Too Tough to Die," you have to expect that some of its former residents were just that. Still, even if you don't come away with any activity, you will come away with a good sense of history, a pleasantly full stomach and probably an "I'll be your Huckleberry" T-shirt or two. Not a bad trip by any account.

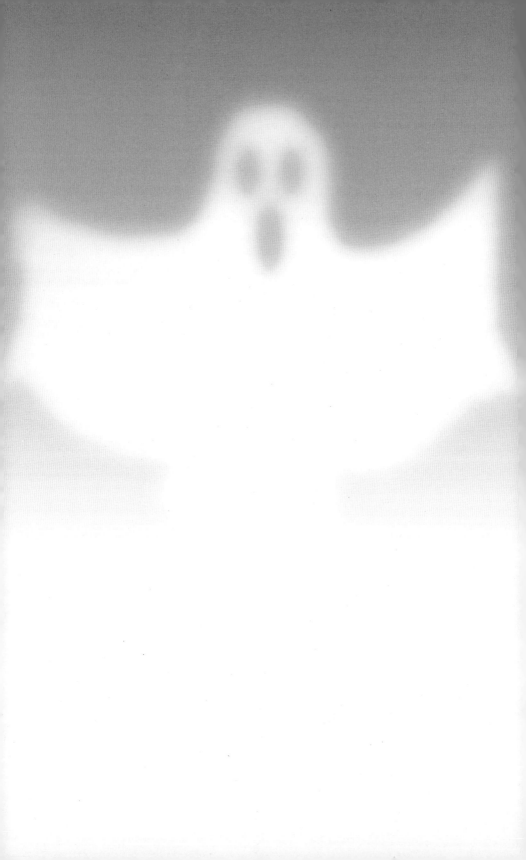

SECTION FOUR:
OTHER SCARY PLACES

PIONEER PLAZA

The Pioneer Plaza is situated in the middle of downtown Tucson, a newly renovated business office at the heart of the city's revitalization effort. Housing several professional offices, one would hardly guess that this was the site of Tucson's most notorious and horrific tragedy.

Once located in the exact spot of the business office, Pioneer Hotel was the absolute epitome of Tucson's high society. Everyone who was anyone had visited the hotel, from cowboys to dignitaries. The hotel was especially bustling one busy night in December in 1970. The full house of hotel guests had come from all directions to take advantage of some last minute Christmas shopping, and several hundred employees of Hughes Aircraft were having their annual holiday party. The festivity soon took a dramatic turn at the discovery of smoke and flames. Pioneer Hotel had been deliberately set ablaze. The otherwise lavish hotel had a woefully inadequate contingency plan in the event of a fire, and the very design of the hotel – with its open stairwells and flammable carpeting – actually fed the flames. Guests were trapped in the upper floors with no way to escape. Some, operating on sheer terror, threw mattresses from the windows onto the sidewalk below, then jumped from the windows, hoping the mattresses would break their fall. Most of those people died on impact, while others suffocated in their rooms. Even the hotel's owners, Harold and Margaret Steinfeld, were not spared from the tragedy. Both were found dead in their penthouse apartment, a result of smoke inhalation. In the end, twenty-nine people died in what remains Tucson's single greatest loss of life, and although many decades have passed since the tragedy, there are still countless people who remember exactly where they were the night of the Pioneer Fire.

Since the reopening of the business complex, there have been numerous reports of smoke smells filling the air with no sign of fire. Also reported are sounds of screams that have no earthly origin. Many times I have passed by the building and seen a fire truck parked in front and found myself wondering the nature of its presence. Although the hotel is gone, clearly it will not allow itself to be forgotten.

UNIVERSITY OF ARIZONA

When the University of Arizona opened its doors on October 1, 1891, it consisted of one building — Old Main. Since that time, the university has grown in size to a 387-acre campus with 182 buildings and over 36,000 students. Probably not counted in that statistic are the ghosts of students that are alleged to remain on the campus long after their passing. Reports of paranormal activity on the campus have been circulating for years. Although there are numerous variations of the stories that abound, the basic information remains the same.

As mentioned, Old Main is the oldest of the buildings on the campus, so it would not be unheard of for such an old building to have a little ethereal residue. Although the specifics of this particular activity are not easy to pinpoint, the custodial staff has reported hearing strange knocking sounds, seeing apparitions, and feeling the icy cold touch of ghostly hands.

The Maricopa Residence Hall is also said to be haunted. Allegedly, a young girl committed suicide in the basement of the building before it was used as a dormitory. Reports of activity have surfaced over the years, mostly from students who have described seeing the girl roaming the lower hallways.

Perhaps the most notable of the hauntings at the university is the report of a young woman who remains bound to the Modern Languages building. Some reports tell of a girl in a flowing white dress on the third floor while others describe her as an ill-fated athlete, running desperately to escape her attacker. As the story goes, when the Modern Languages building was being constructed, the crew uncovered an old well. Contained in this well were the remains of a young lady who had been missing for many years. Some reports even expound upon this story, alleging that the location was once the site of a running track where the young woman was murdered and her body concealed inside of the well.

WESTWARD LOOK RESORT

The Westward Look Resort is nestled snugly in the very exclusive northwest side of Tucson, an enduring landmark with a history steeped in southwest opulence and sturdy tradition. Families that visit this resort stay for weeks and months at a time, and return year after year.

What started as a 172-acre homestead built by William and Maria Watson less than one year after Arizona became a state has grown into a world renowned resort and spa, boasting 244 comfortable and airy guest rooms, a rooftop terrace for watching sunsets, and an award-winning chef who prepares meals with ingredients grown on the premises in the delightful "chef's garden."

The original living room is still featured prominently in the common area of the resort, decorated with numerous vintage photographs depicting guests from bygone eras engaging in all manners of seasonal merrymaking.

The story takes a bit of scary turn down a dark road. According to legend, a young bride was residing on the premises (it is unclear whether she was a guest of the resort or a guest of the Watsons) and, shortly after her long-awaited nuptials, she found her new husband engaging in an adulterous affair. Devastated by this revelation, the young lady once again donned her wedding finery, climbed a large tree in the adjacent courtyard, and promptly hanged herself.

Although this story is not one that is routinely circulated to guests of the hotel, it is significant enough to mention to employees during their training. One former employee described her own run-in with the ill-fated bride. Late one evening, after her shift had ended, she was using the outside restroom a short distance from the courtyard that houses the aforementioned tree. Alone in the restroom, she approached the sink to wash her hands. As she reached to turn on the faucet, she heard the distinct sound of high-heeled shoes walking across the echoing Saltillo tile floor. Aware that nobody had entered the restroom after her, she forced a tentative glance over her shoulder, which confirmed that she was still "alone." As the steps moved closer, she quickly washed her hands and ran from the restroom. No one followed her out.

Another former employee of the resort was working one evening in an upstairs office. He stepped out of the office into the adjacent restroom, leaving the office door slightly ajar. In the brief moment he was out of the office, he distinctly heard the screeching sound of coat hangers being dragged across a closet rod, followed by a loud slam against the wall. Stepping quickly back into the office, he found that no one was there and nothing had been disturbed.

Other experiences that have worked their way into the lore of the hotel include an employee — alone in an executive meeting room — preparing coffee and tea for an upcoming meeting who was startled to hear the sound of a lady's voice saying "Mmm...

coffee." Certainly not as frightening as hearing demonic voices demanding that you vacate your home, but disturbing enough to cause a chill down your spine and to question your own sanity. Probably the most fantastic experience that gets circulated in the allegations of paranormal activity is the incident involving a long-time employee of the hotel who was setting up one of the meeting rooms when all of a sudden...all of the pens that had been placed on the table stood upright as if to scrawl some ghostly communication, and just as suddenly, all of the water glasses spontaneously shattered.

THE END OF THE ROAD

Well, that was quite a trip. What have we learned? For one, obviously Arizona is chock-full of haunted places. What we've experienced with you is a slice off the top of a very large apple. There are dozens more places to visit, and every time you go out and talk to people at haunted places you are going to find even more. We have shown you the most prominent and the most accessible, and we've given you some foundation upon which to build an entire lifetime of knowledge. You should be able to strike out on your own with the confidence that you too can investigate paranormal activities and not just sit on the sidelines watching it on TV.

It is a big world out there with a lot going on that we don't understand. There are those who are content to let others sort it all out, but now you don't have to be included in that group. You can and should be right out in the thick of it. Now, to be clear, you aren't equipped to publish any scientific papers and challenge the skeptics with your hard data. You will need to get quite a bit deeper into the science for that. There are numerous resources available, from college courses to training programs. If you choose to take that route, now you have some experience to take with you.

If you choose to stay on the casual path, that is fine too. You have the keys to the car and you can drive it wherever you want. As always, obey the laws of the road. Be respectful, patient, and professional. Don't speed or trespass and watch for the road rage. Another group may make some illegal lane change, but that isn't your problem. They can get the ticket while you make it safely to your destination. There is always going to be someone doing the wrong thing...just make sure you are doing the right thing. Eventually, they will reach the pinnacle of their ability, and you will move ahead.

There may be groups out there that try to tell you that you are lesser because you are just starting out, or that you don't know what you are talking about or you don't have enough experience to investigate. Everyone started somewhere and that starting point doesn't have to be in their expensive certification program that requires that you sell a kidney and your first-born just to make the tuition. Is training for a group automatically bad? No, but knowledge in this field is based largely on experience gained on an individual basis. Groups that may try to enlist you based on their belief that you don't know enough can save their breath and your time. You are no less valuable to the study than they are and now you have some tools to continue your search for paranormal activity. Use that to your advantage and make your own way. If you are respectful, professional, and have paid attention to the tools we've given you, then you will rise with the rest of the cream.

If one thing should be clear, it is that there are many different experiences out there and everyone experiences them differently. Just remember that finding something new is not unheard of, but results may not always be legitimate phenomena. The howling you hear in the night could just as easily be a faulty air conditioner whistling through a squirrel's nest, so remember to rule out the common, more mundane causes for something before leaping to the conclusion that there is anything paranormal going on.

Many hardcore skeptics claim that they believe what they can feel and see. Hopefully by this point you have done just that. Can you prove it? Probably not, but if you are doing this for experience sake, then that is all the proof you will need. On our walk-throughs we have shown you how we investigate and how we react to activity. You have seen some places that were really active and some places that were relatively quiet. This should give you a good idea how results can be interpreted. Don't dismiss things because you think you are being silly. Write it down, check it against what has been reported, and see how you did. If your experiences are similar, then you have some direct hits; if they aren't...better luck next time. You aren't always going to get a fantastic result, but the point is to keep investigating. Trust yourself and your instincts — and document extensively. You'll learn to discern between legitimate evidence and what might just be the chili cheese dog you had for lunch. It is trial and error, and sometimes it takes a while to get the hang of it.

In summation, make sure you go out with a good attitude, a good night's sleep, keep yourself sober, and have fun. You don't have to be a psychic, a super-hero, or the chosen one to investigate paranormal activity. You need an open mind, a pocket full of skepticism, and a healthy dose of professionalism. Don't let anyone tell you that you have to be born with a gift, have a near death experience, or some traumatic event to be able to investigate the paranormal. You know the basics, you have some experience, and you can do it. We believe in you as much as we believe in the activity we are hunting. Now...get out there and start investigating.

RESOURCES

http://oire.arizona.edu/UAFactBook.asp
www.colossalcave.com
www.crystalpalacesaloon.com/history.htm
www.legendsofamerica.com/az-tombstoneghosts.html
www.nelliecashman.freeservers.com
www.westwardlook.com